Leominster in Living Memory

Leominster in Living Memory

compiled by

Malcolm Mason

Logaston Press

LOGASTON PRESS
Little Logaston Woonton Almeley
Herefordshire HR3 6QH
www.logastonpress.co.uk

First published by Logaston Press in 2010
Copyright © Leominster Museum 2010

ISBN 978 1 906663 43 8

Typeset in Minion Pro by Logaston Press
and printed and bound in Malta by Gutenberg Press

Contents

Acknowledgements

At the end of any project it is always a pleasure to be able to thank the many people who have helped in so many ways to make working on it such a pleasure.

The idea for the project originated in outreach work carried out by the then curator of Leominster Museum, Lynne Moult. A committee was formed with Michael Bloy, secretary, Geoffrey Crofts, chair, and Mark Richards, treasurer, to develop the project and guide it through its formative stages. Later Richard Wheeler took over as treasurer, and dealt with the complications of the budget and submitting accounts with great efficiency. Much of the day-to-day work on the project fell to Michael Bloy, a task to which he has devoted countless hours.

This project and book would not have been possible without the generous support of the Heritage Lottery Fund. Special thanks must go to Lucy Caruana, our Project Officer, for her sound guidance and care.

Other volunteers and supporters of the museum also provided help and advice. Thanks to Christopher Bradbury who took over from Lynne as curator, and to volunteers Terry Collier, Bev Hicks, Peter Jones, David Hinds, Frank Low, Elizabeth Lewis, the late Maurice Lewis, Frank Low, Brettina Meadows, Peter Reed, Wendy Sladen, Eric Turton, and Denis Turton. Special thanks to Mary and Richard Wheeler for finding artefacts for the handling collection and sharing their extensive collection of postcards and photographs. They, together with Christine Evans, have provided practical help and encouragement in equal measure throughout the project; their kindness and friendship are much appreciated.

The interviews were carried out by Malcolm Mason, Tony Overton, Joan Thwaites and Annie Gambol, and transcribed by Malcolm Mason and Gwenda Causer.

The project was supported and advised by officials at Herefordshire Council. Thanks are due to Judy Stevenson, Senior Collections and Access Officer, and Museum Development Officer Virginia Mayes-Wright and her successor Sue Knox, Rosemarie Fleming of the Schools Library Service, and Elizabeth Semper O'Keefe of Hereford Archive Service for their help.

I am grateful to Pauline Davies, Minnie Davies, Roy Gough, John Hinton, Herbert Millichamp, Fred Parsons, John Sharp and Stanley Yapp for permission to use photographs or quote from their written accounts. I have tried to contact possible copyright owners of other material used, and apologise for any infringements I may have committed inadvertently. The quotations from members of the Hallamshire Battalion are taken from *Polar*

Bears from Sheffield by Don Scott, published by Tiger and Rose Productions, Sheffield, by kind permission of Don Scott and Mary E Hart-Dyke.

I would like to sincerely thank all the residents of Leominster who helped with the project, and greeted requests for interviews or other material with unfailing patience and hospitality. My apologies to those whose recollections have not been included in this book. I would especially like to thank Pauline Davies and Meryl Boff for their help with this work. Thanks are due to the staff and residents of Ashfield House, BUPA Care Homes, Forbury House, Norfolk House and Waverley House, staff and members of ECHO Leominster, Gerry Burslem, Linda Crichton, Linda Glover, Peter Holliday, Peter McCaull, Kay Mellish, Gill Owen, Nick Wallis and Richard Westwood.

leom*in*ster museum

Leominster Museum opened to the public in 1972. It is housed in a former Mission Hall in Etnam Street and welcomes over 3000 visitors a year to view its varied displays recording the history of the town and the surrounding area. The museum is managed and staffed entirely by volunteers, and relies on donations for its funding.

The museum is open on weekdays between Easter and October.

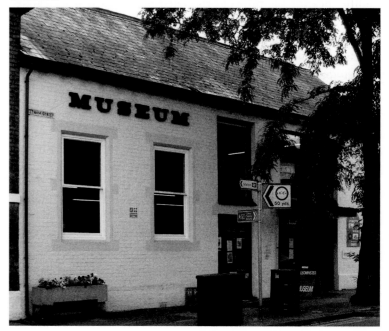

Introduction

Leominster, in common with other market towns in Herefordshire, saw many changes in the last century. During this time the population of the town more than doubled and many of the traditional industries closed. As transport became easier people started to travel to work and shop elsewhere. The close relationship between the town and the surrounding countryside altered, the changing seasons no longer brought traditional festivals and celebrations, and the days when country dwellers could pass a whole lifetime without leaving the county are long gone.

But what has it been like to live in Leominster during this time? There are many questions to ask. From the simple things in life, like changing gas lighting to electric, to the more complicated – how did people find work? How did local families respond to the ebb and flow of life around them? How did the decisions made by movers and shakers change the lives of ordinary people and their families? This is what this project based in Leominster Museum set out to record. We began by talking to people in Residential Homes; some of these interviews were recorded. We also talked to other residents in the town, recording their stories and collecting photographs and written accounts to add to the material already available in the museum. The written accounts, notes, original recordings and a verbatim transcript of the interviews have been preserved without editing, and all of this material has been deposited in Leominster Museum and the Archive Office in Hereford to form a permanent record for future generations.

It is this material which forms the basis for this book. Written out in full the transcripts would fill nine books of this size, so material has had to be selected. To bring the strands of a story together, or to make the meaning clearer, it has also been edited. To maintain readability these edits have not been marked in the text, but in all the editing great care has been taken to preserve the voice and meaning of the interviewee and avoid distortion. The accounts have been grouped under headings and arranged broadly in chronological order. In order to complete the thread of a story some accounts have been grouped by theme rather than time. Apart from that I have let the interviewees tell their own story.

This is not a history of the town, it is too selective for that; nor is it a history of drama and intrigue. It is a collection of impressions or snapshots, stories that remind us of the things we have lost, and also remind us that some things have remained the same in spite of change. It is their ordinariness which is so fascinating.

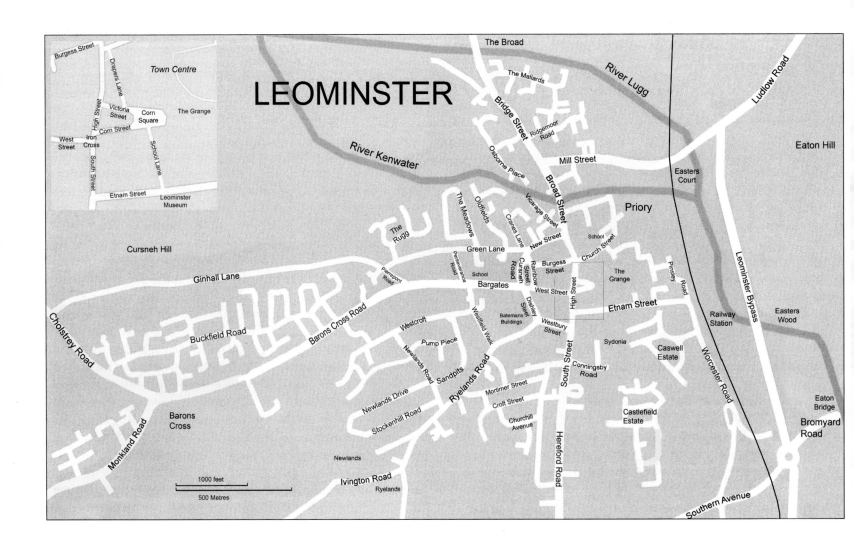

LEOMINSTER

The Broad

River Lugg

Ludlow Road

Eaton Hill

The Mallards

Bridge Street

Ridgemoor Road

River Kenwater

Osborne Place

Mill Street

Broad Street

Easters Court

Priory

Leominster Bypass

Oldfields

Vicarage Street

Cursneh Hill

The Meadows

The Rugg

Green Lane

Cranes Lane

New Street

School

Church Street

Ginhall Lane

Pierrepont Road

Perseverance Road

School

Rainbow Street

Cursneh Road

Burgess Street

The Grange

Pinsley Road

Barons Cross Road

Bargates

West Street

High Street

Etnam Street

Railway Station

Easters Wood

Buckfield Road

Westcroft

Westfield Walk

Batemans Buildings

Distley Street

Westbury Street

Sydonia

Caswell Estate

Worcester Road

Cholstrey Road

Pump Piece

Newlands Road

Sandpits

Ryelands Road

Mortimer Street

Conningsby Road

Eaton Bridge

Newlands Drive

Stockenhill Road

Croft Street

South Street

Castlefield Estate

Bromyard Road

Monkland Road

Barons Cross

Churchill Avenue

Hereford Road

Newlands

1000 feet

Ivington Road

Ryelands

500 Metres

Southern Avenue

Town Centre (inset)

Burgess Street

Drapers Lane

Town Centre

Victoria Street

Corn Square

The Grange

High Street

Corn Street

West Street

Iron Cross

School Lane

South Street

Etnam Street

Leominster Museum

Part One
Before the War

As Leominster entered the twentieth century agriculture was still the foundation on which the economic prosperity of the town was built. The rich farmland of Herefordshire provided a wealth of produce and livestock for Leominster markets, reputed to be the largest in England.

Within the town trades developed to serve the needs of the agricultural population, and provided ready employment to its residents.

As the markets and trades flourished the town prospered, but it did not grow as it could never attract large-scale manufacturing in the way that some other places did.

The story of Leominster during the First World War was the same as that of many other communities across the country. Horses and vehicles were requisitioned, food prices soared, Belgian refugees arrived, and women started working in munitions. It is a tale of sacrifice, anxiety and bereavement, which ended with the addition of the names of 123 of its sons to the town's Roll of Honour.

After the war, Leominster resumed its role as a market town. Work was available, even if it some of it was only seasonal and poorly paid, and despite the apparent prosperity of the town during the inter-war years there were some areas of real poverty and hardship. This changed slowly as housing was improved, services were supplied to more streets and houses, and philanthropists such as Sydney Bridge helped provide much-needed facilities such as the hospital and the Sydonia swimming baths and playing fields.

The developments in education, for example, remind us of how much things have changed. In the early 1900s there were only two 'elementary' schools in Leominster; the National (Church) School in Church Street and the British (Non-denominational) School in the Bargates. The Secondary School opened in 1909 to 56 pupils paying £2 per term and 19 scholarship or free pupils. By the time it was renamed the Leominster Grammar School in 1915 it had 185 pupils. Full time attendance at school only became compulsory up to the age of 14 in 1918, and schooling in the town was reorganised, with infants going to the Bargates School and older children to the National or 'Senior' School. Up to the 1940s it was here that the majority of pupils in the town completed their schooling.

Distant memories

My grandad was dead before I was born, but I know he sold shoes, and he used to ride a penny farthing bike round the farms and measure up the farmers' boots, so that he could come back and make them in the shop. He also kept sheep on a little bit of ground he had by the Priory.

Denise Pugh

My granny kept the Workmen's Arms. I've seen a photo of her standing at the door in her white apron. Workmen would stop there, and she would cook them a meal and give them a bed, and sell tea and sugar and things like that. Our mam said that she gave away more than she sold, anybody could go and tell her a tale, she was that soft. But when the old man was in the shop they had to pay, he wouldn't let them off.

Our mam used to tell a story about a little boy. Nobody knew who he belonged to, but somebody had pitched him out and he used to live in the gutter. One night Granny gave him a drink and something to eat, and the next morning they found him asleep under the counter. She took him in, bathed him, gave him clean clothes, kept him and sent him to school.

When he came of age to go to work, somebody from Wales came and claimed him. She said he was her son and she'd left him with her parents. Anyway, the lad said he wanted to go, and my granny let him. He said he'd come back if he didn't like it.

Margery Hunt

My grandfather came originally from Mordiford. He went to London and became a policeman, and that's where he met my grandma. She was a real cockney, born within the sound of Bow Bells.

Lee McColgan

I come from an old Leominster family; I think it goes back to the middle of the seventeen hundreds. My great grandmother was a Preece. A lot of the buildings in Leominster today were built by the Preece family.

Pauline Davies

My grandfather's name was John Gilbert Fisher, and as far as I know he started up in Berkeley in Gloucester. He came up here with his shop to Church Street somewhere round about the First World War. Then he moved into South Street on the Iron Cross, I think it was about 1934.

Ray Fisher

Sharps Yard in about 1911. John Middleton Sharp is third from the left wearing a cap. His brother Ernest is on the far left in the bowler hat. The photograph was taken at the height of the apple season, and there are plenty of rabbits available

My grandfather married well in the 1800s and he moved to Yorkshire with the wool industry. I understand that industry then went through a rough time and he decided to strike out elsewhere. He could see there was potential with Leominster, and so he set up business as a wool merchant on a large plot of land adjacent to the railway station. Eventually he became a general merchant, and used to buy from the local farmers and send it by rail up to Manchester and Liverpool. So coming to Leominster was quite deliberate.

John Sharp

Tom Russell was the overseer in Leominster. I remember him saying that in his time if you sent a letter to somebody in Birmingham, you could get the reply in Leominster on the same day. Leonard Wilkes was Head Postman in the 1930s. He told me he joined as a boy messenger when the Post Office was in Broad Street, where Fletchers the Newsagent are now. Then it moved to Victoria Street, where Barber and Manuel now have their delicatessen. The sorting office was behind it, and is now part of Richards Furnishing. If you go into their workshop you will see a parquet floor, because the Post Office always had parquet for their sorting office. In 1908 the Post Office had the building put up in Corn Square. It was built by a private landlord to PO specifications; his name was Henry Southall, and he was the chap who also built the Leominster Printing Company next door. So in 1908 it moved from Victoria Street to Corn Square, and it was there for ninety-eight years until it closed in 2006.

Doug Lewis

Leonard Wilkes, supervising postman at Leominster. He was presented with the King George VI medal in 1937

My grandparents originated in North Wales. My grandmother came down in service, to the Bargates. My grandfather had a couple of jobs, I believe, and he delivered groceries at one stage. One lady was always complaining that the bread wasn't fresh. So one day he got a stale loaf, saturated it in a spring and put it up on the top of the van to dry. And the next week she said 'I've never tasted such nice fresh bread!'

Minnie Davies

From what I've been told my grandfather was from a very well-off family. They had a farm on the Ludlow Road and he used to breed horses. It burnt down, they lost everything, and they moved to a cottage on the outskirts of Monkland. So Dad was brought up there, and when he was older my grandfather bought the house down in Etnam Street. It's now the Veterinary Surgeon's house.

Meryl Boff

Excitement became intense in Leominster when it became known on Tuesday August 4th that the Territorials were to leave town the next day. The town was awake early on Wednesday the 5th. Before 8 o'clock members of 'F' company were seen making their way to the Drill Hall with their kit, and the enthusiasm with which the men responded to their country's call was keen and sincere.

Leominster Press

I was four when Father volunteered for the First World War. I don't think he went abroad. We never knew why they kept him back, but he worked in the canteens; he had quite a bit to do.

They hadn't started rationing then so you only had what you could get. I remember Mother going into a shop in High Street in Leominster to ask for some bacon – and I was only a little *twt*. I pulled at her skirt, and I said 'Mummy, that man put some bacon under the counter.' He said that it was fat and we wouldn't like it, but mother said she could fry it, and I could have the fat. I don't know what happened, but I had noticed that he'd put this piece of bacon under the counter. That was the First World War.

Elizabeth Lewis

"They kept lots of secrets in those days"

My mother's father, Harry Hunt, was lost in the war. Nobody seemed to say much, they kept lots of secrets in those days, so I don't know anything about him. All I know is that he was quite small, and his death really affected my mother.

Pauline Davies

My mum's first husband was killed in Salonika in the First World War. My dad was in the war too, he'd say: 'In the Army we used to be up to our waist in mud!' He had bad feet when he came out, but touch wood he did come out. He said it was seeing his mates being killed by the side of him which hurt.

Dorothy Oughton

Moulsher's shop in the High Street

My mother's parents farmed just north of the town throughout the First World War. Her father and brothers broke in colts and trained them to pull the big guns on the Western Front.

Roy Gough

My grandfather was Albert Moulsher; he came from Lincolnshire as a manager for the drapers shop in Number 4 High Street and then he bought out the owner in the early 1920s. My grandmother worked in the town at one of the drapers stalls, Bonmarche I think, which was in High Street. She came from the Broad Farm in North Road in Leominster. She remained there during the [Second World] war and my mother was brought up there. They moved back to 4 High Street after the war but because my grandfather had been in the Tank Regiment he was terrified of fire, because he'd seen so many people trapped in tanks. The house at Number 4 is timber-framed throughout and he was always very worried that it might get hit by a bomb or there might be a fire and they wouldn't be able to get out. So he rented a house in Bargates. Not long after that he bought Newlands Croft in Ryelands Road.

Maureen Crumpler

My father worked quite a bit on the farm, and then he went to work in the ammunition factory in Hereford. He did spend some time in the war. He was in the trenches and when he came out, he had what they called 'trench feet'. But he got over it – he wasn't too bad.

Eileen Bacon

We used to have a tramp who would come to our house regularly. Dad always gave him a mug of tea, some bread and a lump of cheese, and sixpence. When I asked my dad about him, he told me that they had been in the army together. He had a home when he went into the army, but when he came out his wife had left and taken the lot, so he took to the road. We had a long passage with a door each side, and he bedded down there more than once. Dad gave him a blanket and a bit of straw. Dad said I was not to tell Mother about him because she'd play up.

Margery Hunt

Hundreds and thousands of children were orphaned in this country in consequence of World War One. My father was gassed and wounded at Ypres so he wouldn't have been able to work, even if work had been available. We three children were split up to live with aunts and uncles, never the three of us together. It was a great effort on the behalf of my relations to have us because they had children of their own and money was so scarce.

But my father missed us so much that he had us back to live at Fownhope. Mother died of peritonitis in a little cottage at Fownhope when Clifford was a baby only two weeks old, and we all went to the orphanage in Ryelands Road. Twenty-four boys and twenty-four girls, that's how many were there. Having lost our mother, and then losing our father as well, somebody recommended us to a huge orphanage in Bristol. They could accommodate 2,200 children. And so we were there, but we were separated. I was allowed to see my brother and sister only once a month, on a Friday for one hour per month. It was cruel, wicked.

Alec Haines

The Old Boys have done well. We expected they would, and it is nice to record their deeds. Leonard Roberts was the first to die for his faith and country, and then Leonard Bridge. Afterwards Theodore Mills and now Oscar Griffiths. We remember them as happy schoolboys, kindly and good natured, working and playing amongst us, just typical English schoolboys.

Frank Baker and Wilfred Ross looked in at the school. Both were in the Flying Corps and both alas were shortly afterwards taken prisoners. We kept sending them parcels of food, just to show we were still thinking of them.

Cyril Hart came, he had been "over the top" and had been wounded. He had stopped a bullet he said, but it had not stopped him.

Leominster Grammar School Magazine

Dad [Harley Davies] got chlorine gas, and when he came back from the army the doctor told him he was not to have an indoor job, it would kill him. He heard that there was an opening for someone to go round the country with paraffin, soaps, powders and polishes. So he did that; he must have started in about 1922.

He sold Pinkabolic soap, Matchless Cleanser, Fairy Soap, Lifebuoy, Knights Castile, Palmolive, Lux, Persil, Oxidol, Rinso, and then Omo came onto the scene. Silver Flakes, soap flakes. Candles, soda, toilet rolls, matches. And Fry's cooking fat in a tin. Quite a variety. At one stage, it might sound strange, but he used to sell a cough mixture called White Cross. It was like liquorice – it was beautiful – I could drink that by the spoonful.

He started with a horse and covered cart, or dray or whatever you like to call it. I used to go out with him, I always enjoyed that. Then he went on to a van, just before my brother was born in 1933. I used to love going with him on the van. Mondays we did Stoke Prior and Hamnish, Tuesdays Kingsland, Wednesdays Luston, Berrington and Eye, Ashton and Kimbolton and back into Leominster. Thursdays Bircher, Aylton and back in, Leominster on the Friday, and Saturday was Monkland, part of Dilwyn, Hyde Ash, Ivington and back into Leominster. He always said that he wouldn't be out after dark. He arranged the rounds so that he was back in Leominster in daylight.

Minnie Davies

My mother grew up in Leominster, opposite the Bargates School. She was the eldest of three brothers and three sisters. They used to more or less drag her across to school, she didn't want to go, but she was extremely hard working and a great saver. When she was a little girl she saved and bought a bicycle, which was unusual in those days. Her brothers and sisters told me she used to sell rides on the bike for a penny! In those days there was a sweet shop called Henners next to the school in the Bargates, and she went to work there when she left school – she would have been about thirteen or fourteen – until it was found out she was giving sweets away to her friends. That put an end to that!

Pauline Davies

My mother came from the Ross area but my father was born here in Leominster, I think. Because in the First World War there was

Harley Davies (Minnie Davies's father)

a shortage of manpower, he left school earlier than he should have. He started on a paper round with the Orphans Printing Press when he was just twelve. By the time he was fourteen he had full time work with the press. Eventually, in about 1938 he became manager, and he was with them until his retirement in about 1980, so he was there for a total of 66 years. When he started there it was still very much linked to the Quaker Orphanage on Ryelands Road. Then, just before the Second World War, the Press was sold to someone else, and within a few years it was sold again and again. So my father saw quite a lot of changes.

Mervyn Bufton

My father took over Sharps Yard from my grandfather and had a very difficult time in the latter part of the 1920s when the business was on the point of going bust. My father's foreman agreed to put money into the business. That saved it, but all the land was made over to him. After Father died in 1943, the business limped on for about another five or six years, and then it closed down. The gentleman in partnership with my father was Neesham, and when he died the land was taken over by his son, who arranged for a filling station to be developed on the site.

John Sharp

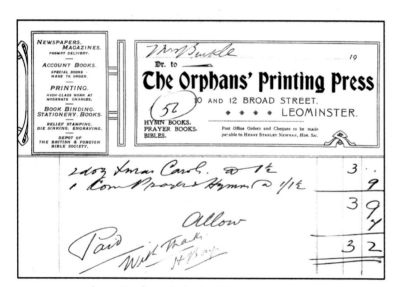

Orphans Printing Press receipt

J.M. Sharp advert

Father was a butcher, when they wanted him. The shops would stay open until midnight on Saturday night as they'd got to sell all the meat, it couldn't be kept. Father had 18 shillings a week and a pound of sausage to bring home on Saturday night. That was our Sunday dinner for a number of years, and we were glad of it! Unbelievably glad of it!

Malcolm Newman

My father was a timber haulier. In those days they used to bike to work, sometimes they'd go several miles. He was a very skilled axe man, he had climbing irons and a strap, and he could go up a tree like *that*. They cut the boughs off, and then it went to the sawmills. His mate, his friend like, would come across on a Sunday afternoon and they would sharpen the axes on a grindstone.

Arthur Evans

My father was an agricultural worker, he was skilled at hedge-laying and caring for sheep. He looked after all the sheep on the farm, the lambing. They'd go to the sales in the autumn and he'd come back with a new flock of sheep – drive them perhaps ten or twelve miles.

Herbert Millichamp

My mum was an angel. She used to work from morning till night. When she finished work at Moreton Camp and came home, she got the meal for us, and we were a big family. Then she would come out in the fields and work, picking up potatoes or strawberry picking, pea picking, all that. Only just down Bridge Street it was.

Eileen Bacon

Eileen's mother was special, she was a special lady. She worked all the hours there were, and when she came out of the fields she used to cook for neighbours and friends, most beautiful cooking. If anybody had a baby, she used to make sure they had a matinée coat. It wasn't just for her family; it was for everybody around her. She was one of those little ladies that was a marvel.

Meryl Boff

"My word, they've got a car!"

After the war my father worked in the Post Office. I think he was in Birmingham for a while, then Llandrindod, and finally Leominster in about 1922. At that time accommodation was very difficult to find. They rented a little cottage down at the bottom of Ryelands and it was not very suitable, so he had a house built at Caswell Terrace, and we moved there in about 1924. We were fortunate. The Post Office was a steady job, so he had a regular income. We didn't have a motor car, though; they were few and far between. If someone had a motor car you really opened your eyes, you know – my word, they've got a car!

Doug Lewis

My dad was born and bred in Leominster, as I was. He was a stonemason at Watkins' at the Tanhouse in Bridge Street. He learned his trade there, and he was there all his life. He used to do the coffin plates and sign writing – he was very clever.

He would give Mum his wage packet, and he did jobs like crazy paving to get his own pocket money. Mr Harvey, who kept Harvey's shop, lived up the Bargates in one of those big houses towards the top. Dad did his yard for him. Trouble was, Mr Harvey wouldn't let anybody walk on it, he was afraid they'd damage it. When their boys used to come to bring the groceries and meat, he'd say: 'Have you got nailed boots on?' 'No, Mr Harvey.' 'Well, good job, because if you did you'd have to take them off!'

Dad used to save his own money in a tin, and we could never find out where he put it. Bert, my youngest brother, knew, but he wouldn't tell anybody. One day my youngest sister had pneumonia bad, and of course she didn't go to hospital, she had to stop at home. The doctor told Mum to put a fire in the grate and put a kettle on the side and let it steam, so the steam would go out into the bedroom. Mum was lighting the fire when Bert came in and stopped her because he knew Dad's money was up the chimney on a little shelf! Dad had to find a different hiding place. We often laughed about it.

In those days they didn't wear masks or anything. Chiselling the stone, the dust got on Dad's chest, and he died when he was 57. He had earned good money, so times were hard for my mother after he died.

Margery Hunt

My grandfather was a barber and my dad followed in his footsteps. Mum was from the London area, Croydon. My dad was sent to London to work for someone else, to gain experience in his trade. Part of his job as a young barber was to go to a hospital and cut people's hair. He was cutting this chap's hair one day in hospital when this young lady came in to talk to the patient; she was his sister. Dad chatted her up, and she became my mum!

Ray Fisher

The first Lord Cawley came down from Lancashire, and my father came with him. He was at Berrington Hall for fifty-odd years. In the house there was a butler and a footman, housekeeper and housemaids, kitchen maids, cooks. He met my mother there; she worked in the Hall as a cook. Outside there was a head gardener, and about four or five under-gardeners. There was the farm, the parks, and one or two fields besides. They had a head groom and two lads working in the stables. They had racehorses, and a keeper who had a house down by Berrington Pool, an estate agent and a clerk. Everybody worked on the estate, more or less. They all had a cottage or a little house; there were five lodges round the main house where people lived. Berrington Estate went from Kimbolton, Stocktons Cross, right out almost to Brimfield, and from the railway out to the other side of Kimbolton.

Lord Cawley's cars and drivers at Berrington Hall in the 1920s. Fred Parsons' father is on the right

Every week my father and the estate agent used to go into town in the Model T Ford to collect the wages from the bank. They used to take it out to the estate office, and the workers came there to collect their wages. Every year the farms around the estate, I think there were about thirteen of them, had to come and pay their rent. They all gathered in the square, and they used to go and pay their rent into the office.

"It was never the same again after the Great War."

My father, being chauffeur, had to wear a uniform, and he used to go to the gents' outfitters where Barber and Manuel is now and get measured for it. He was like me, very short, and he wouldn't have been able to get anything off the peg! It was all made to measure. Lord Cawley was going back to Manchester on business quite a lot, and he had to make an impression when he went back, so he needed his chauffeur to be smart.

I went to the little school at Moreton Eye – I think there were forty or fifty children then. The Christmas parties were wonderful. Every Christmas we used to get a present. I used to get a special book. The Wonder Books: *The Wonder Book of*

Science, The Wonder Book of Railways. There were lots of children – in the villages like Ashton there was the blacksmith and the wheelwright and others, and they all had children. They were all involved with the estate really.

Lord Cawley lost his sons in the Great War. Berrington Hall did carry on but eventually different farms were sold off. It was never the same again after the Great War.

Fred Parsons

Home

There was no central heating in those days. Father spent many hours chopping wood – he'd always carry a stick home from somewhere to cut up. We had a tin bath – two or three of us in the same water, one after the other. When we had pigs we used to cut them up in the same bath! Next time we used it there were bristles round the bath.

Arthur Edwards

We moved to 31 Croft Street; I was 6½ when I first went up there. Not have to go in a tin bath in front of the fire; it was, well, magical really. Everybody wanted to run the tap, and go to the toilet all the time, and pull the chain. It was marvellous to have a bath with running hot water! Everybody wanted to dive in. Children today take it for granted, but to see that for the first time ... people don't believe it, but to us that was a miracle.

Dorothy Oughton

We rented our house from Ross's, the shoe shop people; they lived in the big house at the end of Perseverance Road. They had been tied cottages in earlier times, and my parents got one of them. Looking back, the house was too small for four of us really. There was no bathroom, and no indoor toilet. But the quality of a house is only partly determined by the building itself. Half the value is the surroundings, and from that house we could be out in the open fields within two minutes. We had a world to explore almost on our doorstep, because in the quadrangle of Perseverance Road, Bargates, Green Lane and Pierrepont Road there are large spaces of gardens and trees. It's a wonderful habitat for boys. For birds too, of course – no lack of birds, a great variety. Yes, the outside of where you live is a great asset.

Mervyn Bufton

We lived in a two up, two down in Mill Street. That's where I was born. I was four when we moved from there into Bridge Street, to a three-bedroomed house, the second of four little cottages in the street. There was a passage, and then four more cottages belonging to different landlords. Two rooms downstairs, a little front room and a big kitchen. From the kitchen there was a door that led out the back, but it was all under cover, it was like a little house really. There was a stove in there, a wood-burning stove, or perhaps coke.

We had a built toilet with a bucket seat, but it wasn't a flush one, you had to empty it. When my husband went in the army, my neighbour dug me a pit and put a piece of galvanised metal over it right at the bottom of the garden. That's where I used to empty it and clean it. He did it one week and I did it the next. It wasn't very nice, but you had to do it. It was all sharing toilets, even if you had a flush toilet. I did that for eleven years. We used to get the rats, 'cos there was a farm building by the side of us. My eldest girl, she was about eight I should think, she came back and she had seen a great big rat on the lavatory seat! She wasn't frightened. I don't know, we used to accept things like that in those days.

There were some very nice houses down Bridge Street, but there was some poor housing as well. How people lived in those houses I don't know. Mind, the rents used to be about four

Bridge Street, showing the railings along the River Lugg

shilling a week. But the people was happy enough. In the end the authorities condemned them and built all these new houses, and they wanted to move the tenants from their old houses, but they didn't like it, they didn't want to go.

Margery Hunt

Washing was just as white, I would say even whiter, than the best there is today. The River Pinsley ran along Vicarage Street, and there were washing stones, certainly in the last century. When we were living with my in-laws there was a big boiler in the corner in the back kitchen. You lit the coal fire underneath and then the smoke went up through a chimney. Every Monday the washing was done by all the women in the town. If a man lit a bonfire he'd have been murdered.

Then you had a mangle: two circular rollers with a big handle. If the woman put that down a bit too tight, especially blankets, it was a heck of a job to turn it. 'Oh, loosen it a bit!' They wanted to get as much water out as they could so the washing wouldn't be hanging on the line too long. Wonderful. You miss things like that, you really do.

Alec Haines

I remember the river in Vicarage Street. There were three little cottages that you reached by going over a little bridge. Mrs Cook lived in one, and Mrs Edwards lived in another. I used to have to drive a van down there. Hampton Gardens Bridge – I'd drive onto that and then reverse all the way down. Luckily I never faltered.

Minnie Davies

Cottages in Vicarage Street, looking back towards Bridge Street

At the side of Vicarage Street there were rows of little houses, and a river, with little bridges to cross over to get to the houses. When my husband was a boy, he lived in one of them. Then you went up to The Rugg, Hinton's Rugg they used to call it, and there was Hinton's Corn Shop in Broad Street, a big place.

There was the pop shop, where they used to bottle pop and that. When they built all the houses on that, they dug up nothing but bottles, you know, with the marble in the top.

Margery Hunt

Oh, it used to be a picturesque street, Dishley Street, it was lovely. Women, they'd be out there in the evening in the summer, sat in their starched pinafores, with the jug down beside them, hoping that somebody would come and get them a big jug of beer for tuppence.

I was talking to a lady I'd known for years, a lovely lady. She used to take snuff; lots of ladies did in Dishley Street. She said, 'My old man used to look everywhere for his snuff, but I used to put it in the tea caddy. He was too idle to make a cup of tea, he'd never make one, so I could put my bit of snuff in there and I knew it was safe!'

Alec Haines

I can remember so well – New Street, for instance, was a really poor area. Yet they never locked their doors, day or night. You could leave an old bike anywhere for two days, and it would still be there when you went back for it. They were poor people, but lovely families lived down there.

Malcolm Newman

In the old days, people were so poor that when the bottom bed sheet wore out in the middle, the housewife would cut straight down, turn it over, bring new parts into the middle and sew them up. People much wealthier than us did exactly the same. I suspect that today if a child messes up a sheet it's more or less thrown away.

Alec Haines

I can't say that we were poor. We always had enough to eat and clean clothes. Although I do remember one occasion when apparently my grandmother made me a dress, and the little girl who lived next door, Betty Simpson, she came calling for me to go out to play. I came to the door, and I said 'Oh, Betty, look at my new dress! My grandma made it out of one of Mum's!'

Minnie Davies

Mr Sydney Bridge owned quite a lot of property in Leominster. He used to go round for the rent on a sit-up-and-beg bike, no socks, just a pair of pumps. He looked a very poor man. Once he came into our house when we lived down Bridge Street. We were ill, and the floods were out – it used to flood for a fortnight at a time – and Mother asked him if he couldn't let us off this week. The boys had been bad and everything, and she'd been trying to get them a bit of medicine, because you had to pay your own doctor's bills then. And he said 'My dear lady, the Lord will provide' and he scraped the 1/9 off the table into his bag. 'Bye bye.'

Malcolm Newman

We rented a house in Hampton Gardens. They were all owned by a builder from Kington, Deacon. They weren't very expensive, not by today's standards anyway. It was probably a lot in those days, because wages weren't very high.

Our neighbours were Mr Harris, Mr and Mrs Evans, and Mr and Mrs Owen the other side. The Pembertons were the other side of that, Mr Pemberton worked on the railway. There was a Mr and Mrs Smith, Mrs Jones – her husband was killed in the war, and she lived in the end house. There was the postman, Mr Nichols; he lived just opposite. Who else? Mr Breese – he worked at Cadbury's. Mr Griffiths – he was a tailor who worked in South Street. Mr Bassett, who lived down the bottom, had a photography shop in Broad Street. His daughter still ran that until just recently, when it closed. There was a policeman at the top end of the road, Mr Powell, and Mr Beaman – he used to run the cycle shop in Broad Street and went into televisions when they first came out.

Ray Watkins

"They brought bread and milk with a boat."

We used to be flooded out nearly every winter. There was a little stream that went down opposite our cottage, and it would come in and we would be flooded out half way up the front room. It was only a two-bedroomed house, and you can imagine all of us sitting there. They brought bread and milk with a boat, until the water receded. We were flooded nearly every year. I was only five, and we didn't have to go to school when there was a flood, which was lovely. It wasn't nice for my mother, but you don't see that when you're a child. It must have been awful for Mum and Dad, to try and cope.

Mind you, it sometimes used to flood from the Canniter Bridge all the way down Bridge Street. We couldn't go to school then, because our school was in the Bargates.

Dorothy Oughton

*Sandbags protect the doorways
of numbers 21 and 23 Bridge Street in March 1963*

When we lived in Bridge Street, the floods used to come down the back of our house and out through the front door! They had to come and take us up to the army camp because we couldn't go in the house. But I used to live and work in a very posh house, cleaning. They said I was to go there and take my sister Evelyn, who was only little, with me, because it wouldn't be very nice for her to go up to the camp.

Eileen Bacon

There were floods down Bridge Street, and North Road, where I lived. We had it in the garden; we had it for six weeks. We were living upstairs, all the downstairs was flooded. We had to walk on tin cans, we had no wellies. Then the kids went off to the Army camp at Barons Cross. They were excited, they loved it, but I wouldn't go.

Mrs Peatt and a lot of the councillors came down in open lorries with a megaphone. They were afraid that we'd be washed away. I told her I'd get up on the roof! I didn't want to leave the house open. The war was on, so they said the Air Raid Warden would patrol and see that my house was all right.

They used to bring us two meals a day. Something at lunchtime, a drop of soup, and we had our bread, and the warden looked in at twelve o'clock at night to see how it was. Of course there wasn't a telephone to call for help in those days.

Margery Hunt

It used to flood right along Bridge Street. I can remember it flooding six times a year. I worked in the garage down there and it made a tremendous mess. Water got in the petrol tank. When the mud dried out, the line would be six foot off the floor. We used to have three or four or even six floods a year, till Bob Booth took the river north, to go round Leominster – saved all that flooding.

Alec Haines

We had a detached, three-bedroomed house in Caswell Terrace. I remember my father saying that it was one of the first private houses to be built. He went to the electricity company and said he wanted a supply, and they said they would connect us if we paid for the poles, but he said no. There was a local gas company in those days, and they would lay on gas for free. We were on gas for years! We had gas lighting, and in fact it was gas throughout the whole house. In the evening, when we went to bed we didn't bother to put the gas on; we had candles. It was delightful. When I smell the smoke you get when a candle's blown out, it carries me back to when I used to blow the candle out at night. You'd get the smell just before you went to sleep.

Doug Lewis

When I came out of the Army in 1947 there was hardly any electric lighting. There was just one gas light in the middle of the square. It was very eerie to walk about in the evening – wonderful though. We had a man called the lamplighter who had a long pole with a light at the top. He hitched something on the gas standard in the street and that put the gas on, and then he would light the gas lamps. In Vicarage Street, where my brother lived, there was one at each end of the street, but each only gave a small round light on the ground. In the winter the lamplighter would be lighting at four o'clock. All the children would be waiting for him and he'd have a drove of them following him to the next one, so

VICARAGE STREET, LEOMINSTER.

An early view of Vicarage Street, showing the gas lamp attached to the cottage on the right

Gas men in Corn Square

Harry Newman was one of Leominster's last lamplighters. He started work in 1919 and for 16 years was a familiar sight around the town with his bike and oil torch. When the lighting contract was given to the Electricity Company in 1935 Mr Newman continued with the Gas Company in other duties

they could play. It was absolutely marvellous for the children to be able to do that.

Alec Haines

We had gas and electricity, but only gas in our bedroom. Mum would say, 'Be careful with that mantle!' But somehow you made a hole in it anyway, and then the gas burnt in a different way.

Ray Fisher

We had a gas meter you had to put a penny in. Then a chap, a Mr Newman, used to come along and empty them. He would leave ten or twelve pennies in, or give them as a discount.

Alec Haines

When it was dark, Mum used to come up with the candle, but we weren't allowed to keep it. We had gas lighting in there, a little gas mantle, and we would be trying to read and do things by gaslight. My sister was 15 months older than me and very mischievous. The mantles were so fragile, and she used to put a pencil through or something, and I used to get the blame! She was terrible.

Dorothy Oughton

Leominster produced its own gas from coal at the gas works, which today is the Broad Street car park. The coal came from Cannock on the railway down to Leominster Station, and two chaps used to go down and shovel it into a high lorry. Fortunately the lorry could tip up, so they didn't have to shovel it out again. There was what was called a demurrage on the trucks, which meant that if it was still there after a certain number of days there was extra to pay. They'd be working very hard all day to avoid the Gas Board having to pay this excess payment. At the gas works they had a conveyor of cups on a chain, and that would keep going day and night, taking the coal up forty foot to the bunker at the top.

Alec Haines

My uncle worked in the gasworks and we used to fetch the gas mantles from there, for the gaslight. You had to be ever so careful 'cos if you went a bit rough they'd break, and you'd have to go and get another. All the fires would be going. When the kiddies had whooping cough in those days, they used to say you should take them up the gas works, and the fumes from the coke will help them.

Margery Hunt

After the First World War, more people installed electricity. The generators were too small to cope with the increased load, so supply was taken from Hereford Corporation by an 11,000 volt overhead line in 1923. Before then electricity was limited to the centre of Leominster, but with the extra power available the Company were able to increase the area of supply to include the Ryelands and Green Lane and by overhead line and the underground cables to cover more of the main streets. My great grandfather Herbert Spurrier supervised much of this work, and his son Ronald carried on the tradition as foreman electrician in Leominster for many years.

Kate Spurrier-Gieler

Leominster gasworks in the late 1940s

A demonstration by Edwards and Armstrong of new electrical equipment for the home, held in the Institute in South Street in the late 1930s

Going to school

I must have been about five when I went to Sunnycroft Private School, which was in one big room on the first floor of a building in Rainbow Street. It was run by Miss Thomas, a very good teacher. She had a teacher assistant, Ivy Hyett, and they divided the teaching up between them. We sat in rows, and we had a session every day reciting multiplication tables, so you got it drilled into you by rote. For writing, you had books with lines, with an example at the top that you had to keep copying. Then there was reading. She used to gather her pupils round in little groups and you used to have to read. It was basic education, but it was a very good foundation.

Doug Lewis

At Sunnycroft Miss Thomas was very prim and proper, hair in a bun, black dresses down to the floor, and black boots, very old-fashioned. She always walked around with a cane. When she said something she meant it – quite strict, I suppose, in a nice way. She was wonderful!

I think there were about forty-five pupils, aged from three to fifteen. The fees were £3 a term, which in those days was a lot of money. As most of the fathers were in the army, mothers had to work very hard to send us there. My aunt used to have to take me as my mother was always working. At nine o'clock we started with prayers and a few songs; Miss Thomas played the piano. She concentrated on English (nouns and verbs), history, geography, religious instruction, but not maths. We copied from a blackboard. As far as I can remember, we had to pay extra for our books.

During break we just sat in the classroom – we had no playground so we couldn't go out – and drank our little bottles of milk, a third of a pint. We didn't have school lunches. About half a dozen of us used to have our lunches at a café called McEwan's down in School Lane. It was one shilling and a penny, and we had the same thing every day – cheese on toast.

The school was on two floors. As you went in, you had to climb the stairs to the classroom, and on the right there was a floor to ceiling cabinet with birds' eggs, including ostrich eggs. In the middle of the room there was a bay window, and then next to that there was one of those horrible black stoves which we had to huddle round if it got cold. There was one toilet for all of us at the back, down a little tiny passage way and separated by a curtain, which wasn't very hygienic to say the least.

About once a month we went for a walk, crocodile-style, with our boaters and our blazers. We always went to the same place, up

Green Lane. In those days it was just a leafy lovely lane, and there was the army camp on the right. That later became the secondary modern school. So that's the only break we had from being in the classroom.

We did have an end of term test, but there were no parents' evenings. The teaching was very much left to the school and you got your report to say how you were getting on – that was it. The report was a single sheet of paper, with history, geography and all the other subjects, and a list of marks.

The top floor was kept free, and there were cracks *that* wide in the floor. We always felt we'd fall through, it was really dilapidated. I used to play marbles with Pam Lewis in the cracks in the floorboards.

At Christmas time, one of the older girls used to take us and we had our rehearsals for a concert. Once my friend Barbara Price and I we were the 'Bisto Kids'; we dressed up and parents came. We also had a concert in the summer. The concerts were in the classroom, not the room upstairs, because I don't think it was safe, but we would dance up there. Norma Plant used to organise all that, because she went to dancing classes. She used to play the piano and we danced, and we had to stay on after school for our piano lessons. There were quite a few of us that took piano, and my mother made me take the perishing thing!

Pauline Davies

The first day I started at Sunnycroft School I think I was five years old. My father took me in the car and just dropped me outside the door. I didn't know where to go, but I opened the door and there were stairs going up, so I walked up them, and there was a door on the right. I pushed it open and walked in, and there was somebody sitting there. They said, 'Who are you?' and I told them who I was. Luckily they were expecting me. What a terrible thing to do to a child on the first day at her new school!

Miss Thomas, the headmistress, used to close the school for lunch every day, and we used to go to McEwan's or the central café and have our lunch there. Nice, proper lunches. One day my brother kept saying he didn't feel well, so we went back to school. Miss Thomas phoned the doctor, but she just couldn't handle the situation. I remember the doctor was with my brother in the school, and she was sitting on the stairs crying. I think that's why she closed the school, it upset her so much.

Lee McColgan

"School terrified me."

We lived in Cranes Lane, and my first school was in the Bargates. Mother never took us, we went on our own. Five years old, walking up Green Lane and up Blacky Cross, Blacky Lane, through the alleyway with the other kids, and I started school with my Jacky Coogan cap on and my short trousers. The headmistress's name was Miss Maddox, but I couldn't say her name, I used to call her Miss Maggots. She was a very kind teacher, she never bullied me or anything, but tried to help: 'Come on Malcolm'. That's a happy memory, I suppose, but school terrified me, though it wasn't as harsh, as you might think in those days – I'm talking about the 1930s.

Malcolm Newman

I was born in Rainbow Street, number 1, and I went to the infant school in the Bargates. I don't remember much about it, but I do remember that the teacher sat us out in the playground one summer. I had sunstroke very badly, and I remember falling down on the way home from school and grazing my hands. The teacher said she'd never seen such good writing in all the while I was in the school!

Minnie Davies

At the age of seven or eight the school for the likes of me was the one in Church Street. You went there until you were fourteen, and when you left there were jobs for all.

I don't think we used slates. We might have done in my early days mind, but I don't remember that. We had little books, and you'd write with pen and ink. You didn't have your own pen, couldn't afford a pen! Wherever would the money have come from? It would probably be a ha'penny, or a penny! You couldn't!

Malcolm Newman

I had the cane once or twice, but I think I was a pretty well-behaved child; I was well disciplined at home. All the parents of that generation trained their children to respect authority, and you respected what your parents said, and obeyed them. It carried over into school.

Each teacher had what they called the cane book; it was a little grey book. If you deserved the cane for whatever reason, they put your name in the book. At break time you took the cane book along to the headmaster's study and you queued up outside. There were steps going up to it. So you would see a number of poor miscreants with their cane books, waiting. Then you'd be outside the door, and you'd hear 'Whack! Whack!' Mr Burkett would say, 'What have you done?' and then he'd decide how many he'd give you. If it was only a minor offence he'd probably just give you one on each hand. But if it was more than that, he might give two.

Doug Lewis

There were about 350 pupils at the school. Mr Burkett was the headmaster when I was there. If you did something wrong you had to take the cane book and give it to the headmaster. There was usually a queue waiting to be caned, about three or four. I went once. Prior to going into school you always got into line, and I don't know what happened, but I started fighting with another kid. Anyway he blamed me and I got sent in for it. 'What have you been doing, Parsons?' 'Misbehaving in line, sir.' He read the book. 'Hold your hand out …' – only one.

Fred Parsons

We lived behind the railway lines down North Road, and Mr Weyman used to have the control house there and do the gates. Well, he used to shut the gates to make us late for school. The first train wasn't due until nine o'clock but, never mind what time you got there – we tried it early, we tried it later – he wouldn't let us through. There was a little gate at the side but he always shut that gate. He made us late, and if we were late three times we had the cane. So he wasn't a nice man.

Dorothy Oughton

It was so sad; there was a lot of poverty about in those days, the late 1920s. I can recall kids coming to school with ragged clothes. Some had broken shoes, you could see their feet inside, and some came with a bit of a crust of bread, eating their breakfast on the way. They didn't look well nourished. There was no school uniform. You couldn't expect children to have uniform. There weren't lots of poor kids, but there were some. Looking back on it you just feel so sorry that they were in that condition, but those were the conditions prevailing.

Doug Lewis

At the start of the day we all lined up and went into the hall in the old building; it was quite a big room. The headmaster came in, and a teacher named Miss Jones would play the piano and we would sing a hymn. I don't know whether it was the same one every morning. The headmaster would read out the riot act: what was happening, all the news. Then we'd all disperse and go to our classrooms. Mr Jenkins was maths, Mr Seager was art, Miss Jones was general, Mr Wood was the woodwork master. A funny thing happened there one day. That Sid Harris (he was in the football team), I don't know what he was making, but anyway, halfway through the morning, Mr Wood came round, looked at Harris's work and said, 'You want to get some elbow grease on that, Harris, get some elbow grease on it'. About a quarter of an hour later, he found Harris in the store room at the end of the hut. 'What are you doing up there, Harris?' I'm looking for the elbow grease, sir!' Funny how these things stick in your mind!

Fred Parsons

Miss Weaver from Mill Street was a lovely teacher. Frank Weaver was a solicitor; he used to be very good and took the young kids on trips – the poorer kids of the town. Miss Weaver was going to get married, and the week before she left she bought a box of sweets and she gave us all dolly mixtures. We took them home and I kept mine for days, 'cos sweets was scarce in those days.

Margery Hunt

One of our teachers was Bargy Hughes, and he was a nasty man. One day, I don't know what I'd done, but he hit me across my back with that ruler that you mark on the board. If you went home and told Dad, he'd probably say, 'Well, you must have deserved it.' But this time when he saw the mark on my back he said, 'Right, that's it, I'll sort him out.' And my dad went to the school, and he really set into Bargy Hughes. He didn't mind him giving me the cane if I'd deserved it, but not like that, no way. So he didn't hit me again!

My elder brother, George, he was a bit of a bugger! He was always into mischief, but Bargy Hughes never bothered him. I think he knew that if he did, my brother would give him what for!

Eileen Bacon

Bargy welled my arm once for nothing. I was sat between two big girls – I was only little – and they had done something. Anyhow,

28

he came to hit them and I got it the worst. My mam would never go to school. If we had the cane or anything, she'd say, 'Well, I expect you deserved it, and I hope he gave you one from me.' But my dad did make her go up to school about that. Bargy taught me, and he taught my children. Bit of a heathen, I think.

Margery Hunt

Leominster Senior School football team.
Junior Cup 1933, League Champions and Senior Cup 1934.
Back row, left to right: D. Gittins, ? Griffiths, Les Hicks,
Jim Morgan, Sydney Harris, ? Griffiths
Front row: Bobby Hicks, Fred Parsons, Bill Davies, Gordon Powell,
? Davies

Mr Hughes, he was very good. He used to take us to Worcester Cricket ground. I went once. I think there were three or four of us in the dickey seat, one or two in the front. He took us to see a match, and I saw Bradman play.

Was he strict? Well, they used to work him up. This big ruler that he used to use on the blackboard, he used to walk up and down with it, and they all used to cower. That made it worse.

Fred Parsons

One day we decided we wouldn't go to school. We'd have a day off. So we went up Eaton Hill, and sat there, frightened to death. Then we decided we were late going home, so we went and got ourselves home, but it was only half past two. We were thinking it was time to go home from school! Mum knew we hadn't been to school. Of course you didn't dare tell a lie so I told her we'd had the day off. She said, 'Well, don't let it happen again.'

Eileen Bacon

I learned to swim at school. They used to march us from the school up Bridge Street to the baths, which they used to fill from the brook that ran by. I think they put something in it, as I remember it used to be a greenish colour – I don't know what else was in it! The pool was open, covered round with corrugated iron. It had a springboard for diving, and an iron diving platform as well. It wasn't very big but we had swimming lessons down there.

Fred Parsons

We had an open air swimming pool. We had to go with the school. If it was snow, ice or anything else, you still had to go and do your

*A group of swimmers at the open air swimming pool at The Broad
in the early 1930s*

Children enjoy the Sydonia swimming pool in the 1950s

Sydonia tennis courts

swimming lesson once a week. It was freezing cold, but once you got in the water it wasn't so bad. We had to do it and that was that, but we seemed to enjoy it, we got through it. The water wasn't that good, to be honest. If you'd have gone under water I don't think you'd have seen the top! I always used to stay on the top and try to swim.

We liked going swimming. We'd go in the holidays as well if we could get some money to go, because you had to pay. I don't think it was a lot of money. We did go occasionally but not very often. There were the tennis courts there in the Sydonia, and a little changing hut. We couldn't play tennis, though, because you had to pay and we couldn't afford it.

Dorothy Oughton

I went on to the junior school down by the Priory – rather uneventful, as far I can remember. I had a brown gymslip and woolly stockings – they were uncomfortable. I always enjoyed my lessons, especially cookery lessons with Miss Griffiths. I never had the cane, I was never late, and that's where I finished at the age of fourteen and went out to work.

Minnie Davies

You took an exam to get into the senior school before you were eleven. I was a borderline case, so they said, so I had an oral interview at the Grammar School. That was my first taste of going to this place, which I felt was really something – I went there with a bit of awe. I was asked, 'Which is quicker, thirty miles an hour or a mile in two minutes?' I can remember stopping and thinking, and I said, 'They're both the same' – which was the right answer. That's the only question I remember. Thankfully I passed the exam and I got into the Grammar School.

I'm pretty sure that if I hadn't passed the scholarship my parents would not have been able to afford to send me to the Grammar School. The fees were two guineas a term or something like that. I suppose the average wage would be somewhere about £2 10 shillings to £3 a week.

Some pupils would cycle in: there were bike sheds at the bottom of the playground. Some children came by bus from Kingsland, and from Pembridge and Eardisland with Primrose Motors, and some would come by train, from Hatfield and Steens Bridge, because there were stations there in those days. There was also a railway line running up to Pembridge, Kington, Titley, Presteigne and New Radnor, Staunton on Arrow – they'd all come on the train.

Each day we had an assembly after they had marked the register. The headmaster would read something appropriate, a scripture reading, and then we sang a hymn and then there was a prayer. It brought a sense of reverence to the start of the day; everything was quiet, and I think that had a significant impact on children.

You went to your various lessons. It was the duty of one of the prefects to ring a bell for the end of the lesson, and then, after a break, ring the bell again to call everybody back to their classrooms.

T.F. Green was headmaster. He came in 1932 at the same time as I went to school there. The senior master was Vic Randall, he was a mathematician, a good teacher and a very gifted chap. You'd see him going down the street, and you knew that he wasn't seeing what was going on around him, he was solving a mathematical problem. The geography teacher was Miss Rennie; I can remember a lot of her lessons. When she left we had a Miss Viney.

The woodwork master was affectionately known as 'Bong', everybody liked him. He was a Welshman, and had a very warm nature. Apparently, he once sent a boy out who was causing some disturbance. As he went out he slammed the door. So Lee Thomas called him back in, and he said, 'You go outside and when you go out you do not bong the door' and for the rest of his life he was 'Bong'! He was a very gifted chap. He would play the piano in assemblies, and whenever I hear the Sugar Plum Fairy, it takes me back; I can hear old Bong playing it.

"Of course you were slightly rebellious about the school cap."

In Form 2 everybody had to take Latin, taught by a teacher called Miss Donkersley. Not surprisingly her nickname was 'Donkey'. The music teacher was Herbert Crimp, we called him Herbie Crimp. He'd been an operatic singer and at the end of the lesson he would sit down at the piano, and sing Gilbert and Sullivan to us. Then there was a history master, Tom Howard. He was a good rugby player too, and he used to train the school team.

The girls wore gymslips and blouses, and the boys had a blazer, grey trousers, and a school cap. If you didn't wear your cap, the prefects could put you in detention. Of course you were slightly rebellious about the school cap. I used to carry mine in my school bag when I left home, and walk across the fields through the allotments into the school field. When I got near the school I put my cap on. If you were walking up the street and you saw a master, you had to touch your cap to him. If you were a prefect, they gave you a yellow band which was sewn around the back of the cap. That meant you were somebody.

Every week there was a report book in which were recorded the marks I got for each subject during the week – 1 for the best, and 6 for the worst. You also had a mark for attendance and a mark for behaviour. If you didn't behave well in school, you could get what they called an 'Order Mark'. Everything was totalled up at the end of the week, and then you had to take the report book home and get your parents to initial it, so they knew how you were doing. Oh dear, the inquisition if you got Order Marks!

Sport was cricket, of course, in the summer, and rugby in the winter. The progress of the school sports teams was followed very closely. They had fixtures with other schools, like Hereford, Ross, Bromyard and Ludlow. If it was an away game, they would have a coach to whichever town it was. There used to be a sports day, which was quite an event. Parents would come along to it as well, to be spectators.

I left in about October 1937 after I'd taken the Oxford School Certificate. I was always very grateful that I had the opportunity to go to the Grammar School because it enlarged my thinking and broadened my educational horizon. I appreciated my years in the school there.

Doug Lewis

I was delighted to go to the Grammar School. My first headmaster was a Quaker. Towser Green, T for Thomas I suppose, but we called him Towser. He had tousled hair, I think. He left in my second year and was followed by Scarborough – an austere man. Why he was not in the forces we didn't know, presumably because of ill health. He was only 36 when he came, but he looked an old man, he looked as old as the senior master, who was in his 50s. In boyhood, that's old! Scarborough was a very erect, tall man, with a very strong concept of discipline. No nonsense with him. School was serious. In the few years he was there, the tone and achievements of the school rose astronomically, so much so that in his penultimate year, the school had the largest number of pupils ever taking Higher School Certificate and going on to university. Four or five in that year – there had never been more than one at most before.

"School was serious."

Our teachers were good. The senior master, Vic Randall, was a pillar of strength to the whole school, and much admired because he was a good cricketer. Even at sixty he was one of the town's best cricketers. He had been at the school from about 1922. In languages there was Philip Gush. We thought that he probably did some work for the government as a translator. He was young enough to be called into the Forces, but he must have been doing some special work. He was married to a Frenchwoman too, which probably helped with whatever they were doing – with the French Resistance, perhaps. When the war ended he moved elsewhere. He was accompanied and followed by a teacher who was a great asset to church life and to the town as well as to the school. William Penbury became senior master after Randall's departure. These were quality men who were a great strength to the school.

Mervyn Bufton

The scholarship people formed the A classes mainly, and then you had the B classes, who paid to go to school. Father used to write a cheque, I think it was four guineas a term. That was the cost of education. But the scholarship people, they were in the 'A's, you know, the clever ones. Most of the people in my class who got School Certs. either went on with teaching or some, a few, went to University.

John Sharp

We took our eleven-plus examination in those days and went to the Grammar School. That was in South Street. We got our school uniform from Harvey's. We had to wear grey trousers, and the cap was compulsory; I don't think a blazer was compulsory.

Jacky Pinder was our science teacher; he lived in the Pleasance, up Bargates. Mr Randall was our maths teacher and he lived half way up Green Lane. Miss Brown, English. Miss Crow, history, I remember that one of her little things was about the match girls going on strike at Bryant and May's. (Some of the timber for the matches apparently came from Risbury just outside Leominster.) That was one of her little jokes, that the match girls at Bryant and May went on strike!

Was there much difference between the Grammar School kids and the others? I don't think so. I had lifelong friends that went to the other school, the bottom school we called it because it was at the bottom of the town. I don't think there was any outright snobbery about it.

Ray Fisher

Childhood games and holidays

Playing Out

I remember my brothers playing marbles in the gutter in Bridge Street. Then we used to make a hopscotch bed in front of the house, and Mum used to make us wash it off after. We had our skipping ropes and hoops, bats and balls. We'd make our own bats. We never had bikes or anything like that, but we were all happy kids.

Margery Hunt

We'd get the berries off the tree, call them cherries, and pretend to play shop. We'd put a piece of slate on a stone and that was the balancing scales. We didn't have any toys – that's what we used to play with.

We used to play in the street as well. We'd draw hopscotch on the pavement. My dad would get us a big rope off a tea chest and we used to stand one on this side of the road and the other on the other side, and then we'd all be skipping together across the road with this big skipping rope. When cars came we'd just drop the rope and let the cars run over it. We played marbles in the gutter too. We made a ring of marbles and added some in the middle, and then you had to knock them out. If you knocked one out of the middle you won that one. Or you'd throw a marble into the gutter and if your marble hit it, you won that marble. Sometimes it used to go somewhere else; I lost no end of them.

Then we had a top and whip; that was another thing. You never hear of those now, do you? Dad would put a stud in the bottom of it to make it spin a bit better, and we'd paint different colours on it to make it prettier when it was spinning. Dad used to tie a leather bootlace onto a stick for us, and we would hit the top with this and get it spinning down the road and back up.

Dorothy Oughton

I grew up in the Caswell area. It was a council estate mainly, but it was a young area, and there were lots of families with young children. It was a delightful community. There was a great sense of belonging, and everyone was interested in everyone else.

You'd have lots of friends, and we were always out playing in the street. Motor cars were virtually non-existent, but we took interest in cars – if you saw a car you'd know the make. At school we used to collect cigarette cards. You'd swap cards at school with your friends, try and get the set.

Caswell Crescent, part of the housing development in the 1920s

been developed. I had an egg collection and we went looking for birds' nests and collecting eggs. Of course, that's a most forbidden thing these days.

Doug Lewis

We used to play cards – not playing cards. We went round the men who were smoking, and there would be a card in their cigarette packets. All different things – cars, horses, dogs – and we'd play 'throw them up'. We'd put so many across the edge by the fence, and we'd throw them, spin them onto them. If you got it onto those cards, you'd win that card. I've always remembered that. But there was one lot of cards I would never part with, and that was chickens. I used to love these chickens. They were all different colours, and thirty-two different kinds. I'd never get rid of those, but I don't know what happened to them. I think my mother must have thrown them out. I wouldn't play with them, because I thought they were too pretty.

Dorothy Oughton

I asked Mum and she bought us a hoola-hoop to share, we couldn't have one each. That's what we played with for hours on end, to see who could twist it round the longest, and count up the times and all that. We had great fun with it.

We lived in the end one of a row of houses in Bridge Street. There was a big house there called the Prince of Wales, it must have been a pub at some time or other, and there was this wall and then another row of cottages. We used to go out, climb over the wall, tie a piece of string to somebody's door knocker and pull it. People used to come out looking ... I won't tell you some

We used to go walking in the fields, exploring as we called it. Eaton Hill used to be quite wooded at that time. Very often we'd go out there, walk over the hill and generally amuse ourselves. Above Caswell Terrace in those days there was an open field where they built the Sydonia swimming pool. We used to go up there and fly our kites, it was a topping area for playing. There were fields between the Caswell Estate and the cemetery, where the Caradoc Drive and the industrial estate have

of the things they called us! We got reported because it was so annoying. It was fun for us, but I suppose it wasn't fun for people putting up with us.

Eileen Bacon

"I won't tell you some of the things they called us!"

In those days there were a lot of young people in Hampton Gardens, all about the same age. We used to play in the street – football, and soldiers and things like that – and we had the fields. We could go through Vicarage Street, and up by the river there. We spent hours walking, following the river, playing in the fields, climbing trees, getting into trouble with the farmer.

Ray Watkins

We used to like to go to the Grange; we could go and play there for hours, on the slide and that. That got a bit dangerous for me. Once went as a train on the slide and I was the last one, and I didn't go down that way – I went over the top. It was quite a high one, and I was taken home in a push chair.

There were little toilets on the right hand towards the end, boys and girls, and there was a shelter, for if it rained. That's all

gone. If we felt thirsty we'd to go to the little concrete fountain round the corner by the black and white house. It had a tin mug on a chain and you could press a button to get some water. We had hot summers then and we all used to go and have a drink from the fountain. It seems a pity that went.

Dorothy Oughton

In the summer we'd come home from school, have our tea, and then we'd all go down round Eyton. There was a bridge there, and we'd go up on Eyton Common. It was a good way, mind, and there were farms up there. We often used to find eggs that chickens had laid in the hedge and the farmers hadn't noticed.

We used to go to the Sands and take our tea, especially on a Saturday. By Eyton Mill it was, what they called the Slang and oh, it was lovely up there. One day they'd put barbed wire all over the gates, and locked it. So we played up about it: 'They canna take our Sands off us!'

Margery Hunt

We'd walk all over Eaton Hill. It was lovely up there. And we had the Sands down Vicarage Street – that was our Sunday afternoon. A little gate at the end of Vicarage Street, then there was a little bridge to cross over, and a field. You could paddle in there, and if you went a bit further you could swim, but we used to only paddle, 'cos Mum wouldn't let us go in too deep. We'd take a picnic, and play with balls and skipping ropes in the field. Then all of a sudden they just stopped it.

Dorothy Oughton

Children's Playing Field, Leominster.

G.3310.

You could still walk across the footpath and go down by the river, across the footpath, and come out where the entrance to the tip is now. A little girl got drowned over there. That was some years ago. My grandad said he went the day before, and cut all the bushes down, and then the little girl slipped and fell in the river. He always felt awful about that, but it was his job and he was told to do it.

I think this little girl was the first one to be buried at Leominster Cemetery. She had an angel on her grave and the angel's hand had got like a hole in it, and kiddies used to take a flower and stick it in that hand.

Phyllis Manson

I used to love going to my granny's at Westhope Hill. She let me stay the night, and in the morning I would get up, have toast for my breakfast I expect, and then I would go out and walk for miles over the hills. You crossed a road and climbed over the stile, and I used to go to see an old uncle of mine. He fascinated me because he had a big open fire, and he used put a log in the fire and keep pushing it in as it burned. He wouldn't chop the wood or anything.

Eileen Bacon

On a Sunday morning, Mother would get us ready. As the eldest boy, I would take my two brothers for long walks. 'You look after those boys, and don't rip your clothes!' We might go round Cockroft or right up round Ginhall Lane. Mother said we hadn't got to come back until twelve o'clock or thereabouts while she cooked the dinner. When the wood was on Eaton Hill one of our main games was to get a gang of us to go up there to play Cowboys and Indians in the wood. You'd go off in the morning in the holidays, tell your mother where you were going mind, and you'd forget yourself until you went home in the evening. We were so happy playing up there. Happy enough, happy enough.

Malcolm Newman

We used to go up there to play games on Eaton Hill, hiding up in the woods. It was great fun. There were beautiful primroses and violets and all up there. We used to pick no end of them, and then sell them in bunches to the shops.

My youngest sister was only a baby and we had one of these big prams, where the middle used to come out. We'd sit her down in there and go for a walk all down Eyton, and down the Broad. We'd pinch potatoes, swedes, everything, and put them in this pram. When we took her home she'd be up high like that! Mum never had a lot of money, but I used to be frightened to death we'd get caught, but my brother George used to say I'd be all right with him.

Another thing we did that was very naughty, we used to play over the fields and George used to take a little suitcase. It was always me who had to climb up the tree and pick the apples into the suitcase so that they didn't get bruised. Then George would come back and take them and put them in the pram. I was sat up this tree picking the apples, and – I can remember it now – Mr Moore, from Eyton, came. I could see him coming across the field and I thought 'What on earth can I do?' Anyway, I just sat there, I never moved. George and the others had jumped over the gate and gone into the other field. When Mr Moore had gone George

An early view of children playing on Eaton Hill

came back and said, 'You didn't drop those apples from the tree did you? I don't want them bruised!'

George used to play along Eyton Road, back over the gate. He'd skim a piece of slate across the water; it was great fun. Anyway, he was skimming so hard once that he cut a duck's head off. He took his coat off, wrapped the duck in it and said he was going to take it home for Mam – which is what he did. She said 'One of these days you're going to get caught!' – but we did get away with it.

Eileen Bacon

While my sister Jean stayed at home and helped my mother with the gruelling housework and new babies, I spent my spare time as a child minder wandering the fields and woods around the town. In these wanderings I was always accompanied by my three younger sisters, Lena, Barbara and Marilyn. Many were the times that I brought them home soaked after falling in the river, or covered in muck after playing with the cattle at the market – and I would then work hard at avoiding my just reward!

For excitement though, nothing equalled the blacksmith's shop in South Street, opposite the Bowling Green Inn. The blacksmith was a big, rough and good-hearted man in a leather apron, and the clang of his hammer could be heard far down the street. Sometimes he would let us pump the bellows and watch the sparks and flames from the white-hot fire shoot up to the ceiling while he shod a horse, the air becoming filled with the sizzling smoke and sweet smell of burning hoof. Oh, how I loved that smell!

At certain times of the year the road outside his shop would have a dozen or more huge carthorses lined up waiting to be shod and they were fun to pat and talk to. At other times though, a long row of brightly painted horse-drawn gypsy caravans with their packs of dogs would be parked outside for a similar purpose, but we had been warned that gypsies were dangerous people so we kept well clear of them.

Roy Gough

You never had a lot of finery. You'd have a frock, and a white pinner over the top of it, with a handkerchief pinned on to it. The pinner went round and it had little butterfly wings on the shoulders. It fastened up down the back and had a frill round the bottom. You always had a pair of boots, half way up the calf. After I'd had them about a fortnight my dad used to buy metal studs, and put studs all round the sole and on the heels. Then they brought out a brown boot, and it came up to your knee. They used to call it the gypsy boot, but my mum wouldn't let us have them. Sweets were scarce in those days. When I was a little girl we couldn't just go in and buy some. On a Sunday, my dad used to give us a penny to call at Mrs Parker's at the bottom of Bridge Street by the Red Lion, those little cottages there. She used to make brandy balls and brandy rock. Five brandy balls for a penny, or a penny for a stick of rock a foot long. We used to wrap it in paper and screw it round, and we used to have that every Sunday on the way to Sunday School.

Margery Hunt

If you had anything new it was special. As a very special treat I had a little red dress and a pair of white pumps for Easter Day. We lived down Bridge Street, and there was an entrance going up to the fields with these bars across this river. Of course I'd been warned. I was sitting on these bars, with my arms over, and I went splash into the water. My brother George pulled me out by the hair, because it was quite deep and I couldn't get out. He pulled me out and he said 'Don't you tell Mum!' I said 'I won't have to tell her, George, look at me!' We walked back down to the house, and there I was, dripping in red. My white pumps were red, and I thought, 'Mam will go mad!' Anyway she made me go in, take it all off, and go and get a bath – in a tin bath by the fire! I got away with it, but I never mentioned that George had given me a helping hand to get in as well as out.

Eileen Bacon

"I thought, 'Mam will go mad!'"

One of my father's best mates was a chap named Jack Newton from a well known Leominster family, born in the next cottage to them. They were almost poachers, though they never had guns. It was the thing that was done, because people were so poor.

I had only just started school. They were doing something on the river bank and Jack had what they call a crab wire, and I took this out of his pocket. I thought 'I'll catch a fish with that!' Well, I'm admitting to being a thief! So one dinner time I came home from the Bargates school, and I decided to go up to the Pinsley and catch a fish. It was in flood, and I can vividly remember putting in. I hadn't got an earthly but I never knew this, holding this wire in the water. Suddenly I started to slip, and I slipped down into the river. I couldn't swim or anything. I sank in the water, and there was this old man trying to grab me, and he forced me to get hold of the bank, my fingernails digging into it, and I crawled out, and went back down the field and down Cranes Lane to my mother. It's a miracle that I lived to tell the tale.

Malcolm Newman

"It's a miracle that I lived to tell the tale."

We lived down North Road, that's just below where the tip is now. There used to be a level crossing that the trains used to go across, and then there were six houses on the left hand side. We were the first one, number 3. We moved there when I was three. When I was five my sister was going out with my younger sister; she was three years younger than me. I didn't want to go because she was taking my sister, I'd been a bit spoilt because they thought I was the last, so I was a bit jealous, to be honest. When they got to the other side of the road, I decided I wanted to go, and I ran across. There weren't many cars around, but one came over the level crossing and that was it, I was knocked down. I wasn't badly hurt but it went over my thigh, and I had to go to hospital.

Dorothy Oughton

The Weyman family lived on the level crossing, and we were out playing on the opposite side of the road where Mr Baxter had this big field. I was chasing Georgie Weyman and he went up a tree, and the branch broke and he fell down. He had to go to hospital because he'd hurt his back. I got myself in such a state. 'Whatever's going to happen? – he'll die!' But he was all right, just badly bruised. Oh dear, when you think of the things we used to do.

Eileen Bacon

When I was eight and nine I loved children, I was absolutely obsessed with babies. We used to ask parents if they wanted their baby taken for a walk. I can remember going down to the workhouse and taking out this baby. My friend and I took this child out round the Grange.

Pauline Davies

I can remember the workhouse children. They used to come to school; they were always dressed nicely, they had good boots, and they seemed well fed. There was one girl I took to, and I always shared my lunch with her. They had a cooked breakfast of porridge and a piece of bread and butter, and a dinner of stew, but no lunch. She said she had been left on a doorstep, didn't know her mother or her father. She left school when she was 14 and nobody claimed her so she went to work on a farm. She was grown to be a nice-looking girl, and the farmer's son fell for her. His mother and father didn't stop it, they let him court her. They treated her like their own. They got married in the end.

Margery Hunt

Christmas

Christmas was a few sweets in the toe of a sock, an orange and an apple, a few monkey nuts. A turkey? Good gracious, no, never heard of it. If I remember rightly the farmer used to give us a piece of beef at Christmas.

Arthur Edwards

One Christmas our folks couldn't afford anything for us, a present of any kind. I had two uncles; one worked on the railway, the other at the Post Office as a postman. They were quite well off; they used to get about £2 a week! They came up to our house in South Street and brought us each a little lorry filled with toffees, and that was our Christmas present, because our folks just hadn't got any money! You know, there wasn't any money to be had.

Malcolm Newman

At Christmas Mum couldn't afford to buy us toys, but Auntie Betty used to bring us tins of Quality Street. Oh, we thought it was heaven! A whole tin of Quality Street each! They were round tins, the same sort of pattern on them as there is today. We weren't allowed to eat them all at once. We'd have one or two, then Mum would put the lid on, and we didn't have any more then until she told us we could. She'd say, 'Go on, you can have another couple.'

Eileen Bacon

We had a nice Christmas. There was always plenty to eat. Mum reared her own cockerels for Christmas, and we'd have a piece of beef, or a piece of boiling bacon – just plain, never anything fancy. She used to make her own Christmas puddings, her own mincemeat, and all her own pastry. I remember going home from school with my brother and him saying, 'Our Mum's making her mincemeat tonight, 'cos I've been told I haven't got to go out, I gotta go and stone the raisins.' Mam said, 'He's not stoning the raisins, 'cos he eats more than he stones!'

Generally we were given clothes as presents. Perhaps you'd have a new pinner, or a pair of stockings, or some boots. You might have a little toy, but it wouldn't be much, not dolls and dolls' prams and all that ... but we always had a stocking. Many a Christmas morning we woke up at four o'clock to be told to get back to sleep, it isn't time yet. We used to have our stockings, and in the toe we'd have a new penny, if they could get them. You'd have an orange, a cracker, and perhaps a few sweets. If you had a present, perhaps you'd have a box of handkerchiefs, or a top and whip, or a ball. If you got something you was as pleased as anything.

We were pretty lucky because my mother's sister lived in Birmingham, and she and her husband worked for Cadbury's, Bourneville. They used to be able to buy chocolates that had been damaged, and she always sent us a box. We weren't allowed to put our hand in and take them. We had to wait until they were dished out. I used to love Turkish Delight, I always had one – only one mind, there was nine of us to go around.

Margery Hunt

When I was very young, at Christmas I was taken over to Greenlands, the big store in Hereford. You used to go down into the basement and look at the toys. I always remember those family

Christmases with my mother and father. They were lovely, there's no getting away from it. Father's friends used to come to see him, and they would all give me half-crowns to put in my money box.

John Sharp

May Fair

The fair was the event of the year, of course. It always came on May 2nd – that went back to Queen Mary in the 1500s. Once Christmas had gone, aunties and uncles didn't give you birthday presents, they gave you money to save for the fair.

Pauline Davies

The fair was very much looked forward to. Children and families would take bottles and bones to the rag and bone men to get a few pennies for the May Fair.

Alec Haines

Growing up in Luston, the highlight of the year was the Leominster May Fair, especially as it usually fell on my birthday. It was an encouragement to save our few pennies, which didn't go far on the rides and roundabouts. Even at 3d a go, the coconut shy and the airgun stall soon depleted our three or four shillings' precious savings. You'd spend all your money and have to walk home.

Herbert Millichamp

My parents would give me 7/6 to spend, which was a lot of money. I used to think I was a millionaire! The rides were only tuppence or thruppence in those days. We came in on the train so the train fare had to come out of that as well, and we used to buy a bun.

I came in with another kid one day, at about eleven o'clock, I suppose. We walked down Broad Street, and there was a chap there with a card table, and on one side of it he'd got a pylon and an arm with a string hanging down, and a ball on the end of the string. There was a peg in the middle of the table, and you had to swing the ball and knock this peg over three times to win a watch. This kid kept trying and trying. 'Just go like that', the stall holder said, and he was doing it every time! The kid kept on, and he spent all his money trying to win a watch, but he never did!

All the big stuff used to be in the Square, of course – the gondolas and the waltzers, the coconut shy and the shooting booth. I remember those nice big engines they used to drive the appliances. They'd park these engines at the bottom of Broad Street in Vicarage Street, with a little brook by the side of it, to provide the electricity or something or other to drive these various things. Anyway, I don't know what happened but the one time he tipped it over into this brook, and he had a heck of a job getting it out.

Fred Parsons

For the children the great thing of the May Fair was Studs and Deakin's engines. You would hear them from some distance away. They came trundling into Leominster and then they turned down Etnam Street, and went into my father's yard. That's where they parked. Then they took over the Corn Square and Broad Street.

John Sharp

44

May Fair used to have Studs and Deakin's. Studs were like gentlepeople, ladies and gents, the way they used to dress. Their caravan, something broke in there and they went to Watkins' Tanhouse and Dad went to fix it. He said it was beautiful, like a little house, full of glass and china and brass.

They used to have the fair in the square. Deakins had the hobby horses, and Studs had the gondolas. It was like a boat; you sat in it and you went up and down. All the old women used to go in on the May Fair day. Mum would give us sixpence each to spend how we wanted to. Me and my sister used to buy a 'Tisty Ball'. It was a ball full of sawdust, covered in a pretty cover. Then it was put in a bag and it was on elastic and you tied it round your finger and bounced it up and down.

A large crowd gather to see the Deakin's Traction Engine being extricated from the Pinsley Brook in Vicarage Street in 1937

In Drapers Lane the shops used to come out and there used to be stalls. There was Morrows and Hintons, the sweet shops. The fish and chip man used to come out with a stall. Up Church Street there were more stalls. The peacock stall had a peacock that used to go round and stop at numbers. If it stopped on your number you could have a present. Perhaps it would be a big double-jointed doll in a box, or a little three-wheeled scooter, or a tea set or a set of saucepans. It used to be a shilling a go. Once, when my sister had left school and she was working, they had one ticket left and she wanted to take Mam a tea set in a basket. And she did, she won it, it was the last one! Oh, you'd think we were going to give our mam a fortune. She had a cupboard where she had all her china, and she put it up – she never used it.

Margery Hunt

They always had these hobby horses, right on the corner. We tried to look for our name on a horse, to have a go on that one. My dad used to go and have a pint in the Hop Pole, and if we were lucky we would get a penny off him to go on the horses! If we were given thruppence or sixpence, we thought we were in heaven, because for that you could have three or four rides. Towards the church, Church Street, there were all shows up there. The Bearded Lady, the Wall of Death – and boxing up on the top. We used to try and look underneath the tent, but they found out where our hole was the one time and we were told off. But we did it. We couldn't afford to pay to go in, you know, because that would mean we'd miss a couple of rides. We'd go down every night if we could. You'd go but you couldn't go on everything – you'd just walk round and round.

Dorothy Oughton

The May Fair's a bit different now. I can remember the dodgems, the radio cars we used to call them, and the hobby horses, the Noah's Ark. There were the Lightning Swirls too; they still have those, only they're more sophisticated. These cars would spin round on a undulating surface – this way, then that way, and whoof! They didn't go right round, and there was a bar to hold you in. They had swing boats too; you weren't really allowed to stand up in them, but we used to stand up and give 'em a real pull, and they used to go right up. They were very good. They wouldn't allow those today, perhaps.

Ray Fisher

Saturday night at the May Fair in 1936. Along with the Lightning Swirls and the Airways, the popular radio cars filled the Corn Square in front of the Picture House, while in Corn Street the roundabouts catered for the youngsters

They worked overnight to clear the dodgems from the Square. Early on the Sunday, Sylvie and I and a few other friends used to go up and we'd to find all these thruppenny bits underneath the dodgems.

Pauline Davies

We used to go to May Fair, but there were never many rides I could go on ... bumper cars with Dad, that's the ride we all liked. We were all wusses, we didn't like the big rides.

Lindsey Murray

In the sixties, the mayor of the day asked the fair to move out until the bypass was built. But the bypass took thirty years, and the fair didn't come back. Then in 1988 Abie Morris the May Fair boss, got in touch with me asking to come back. I started a campaign, and I had the biggest petition ever in Leominster. I kept lobbying and we filled the Grange Court with about 120 people that wanted it. Of course, there was opposition, there was even a fight! Tempers were high at the time, but they voted for it and in 1990 the lorries rolled in and it was one of the best days of my life. I loved the May Fair as a child, we all did, because that's all we had. When it went on the Sunday morning we used to cry our eyes out because the fair had gone. That's the one thing that I'm always proud of – that I got the May Fair back.

Pauline Davies

Sunday School and Youth Clubs

At one time Leominster was called Little Amsterdam, because of all the churches and chapels in the town. We've obviously got the Priory Church; but we also had the Congregationalists, the Baptists, Plymouth Brethren, the Methodists, the Catholics, the Moravians, the Apostolic, Jehovah's Witnesses, Quakers, Church Army, and United Reform Church.

Alec Haines

Most of the children would only go on special days but my parents wanted me to go to church and Sunday school regularly. We didn't go every Sunday, but we were pretty regular. Church then was a big thing; people don't go to church now like they did then.

Elizabeth Lewis

When I was a boy there were four churches or chapels which have since closed. Look at the one with the spire in Burgess Street, a very beautiful church on the inside, Congregational. They must have attracted a lot of people. A hundred years ago the well-to-do people in the town would have required their domestic servants to attend their church. There were two Methodist churches as late as the 1940s: the one in Green Lane, the Primitive Methodists, and the older one, the Wesleyan Methodists, opposite the Congregational Church. On Sunday mornings, and probably Sunday evenings too, Burgess Street must have been very busy with coaches, the old horse-drawn type, coming to deliver people to those two chapels.

Mervyn Bufton

On the corner of Burgess Street, there used to be a chapel with a chimney up in the middle. All the poor people used to meet there, women in nice starched aprons and men with their caps on. The same families would be there year after year for their Sunday worship, a marvellous thing. Then Reverend Savage came from Africa and he closed it, thinking that those people would go to the Priory Church. But they wouldn't have dared – it had to be Sunday best for the Priory, and they didn't have the clothes.

Alec Haines

We used to go to Sunday school at the Waterloo Rooms at the bottom of Broad Street by the bridge. Harry and George Foster and their sister Amy used to run it. The little children would be downstairs and we went upstairs. Then they moved from the Waterloo Rooms to Brook Hall. We had about an hour; the teacher used to read a verse out of the Bible and would talk about different things.

The Congregationalist Church in Burgess Street

In the summer we had a tea party in the country. We went in a lorry. The lorries belonged to people who attended church – a lot of the farmers used to attend chapel. Perhaps we'd go out to Berrington Eye, or we'd go up to the woodlands at the top of the Ryelands. You could have currant or lemon cake; I used to love the lemon cake. Then there were sandwiches. We didn't have ham then, it was paste or jam. I could have that at home, but it tasted so different there. Then we had races, and whoever won the race would have a couple of sweets.

Mum belonged to the Mothers' Union, and they used to have mothers' afternoon, for mothers to go and have a break and a cup of tea. They used to start about 2.30 and finish at 4. It wasn't a religious thing; they just used to talk and get advice, you know.

Margery Hunt

We liked going to Sunday school. When we lived in North Road we went to the Brook Hall Sunday school, 'cos that was the nearest chapel. Then we went to the little Methodist church up Burgess Street. We had that as well as that one up in Green Lane. There was one down Etnam Street, the Baptist, and then there was the Friendship place, up Burgess Street, next door to Hodges' cobblers. There was a tiny place in New Street as well, that was a long way to go.

After you'd been to Sunday school for a bit, they used to take you on trips. We used to go to the seaside, and that was our holiday. We never went on a week's holiday, just a day trip with Sunday school. They put it on for us for being good at school, and going to Sunday school. We went all over. We used to go to this Apostolic church and we used to sing this song:

Sunshine Corner, it is jolly fine,
For all children under ninety-nine,
All are welcome, seats are given free,
Leominster Apostolic is the place for me.

I've remembered that all my life, it's funny what sticks in your mind. And now it's been turned into a bungalow.

Dorothy Oughton

On Sunday afternoon it was Sunday school at the little Wesleyan chapel, where my dear old teachers Mr Adams and Mr Tomlins faithfully tried to train a child in the way he should go. It must have been difficult for them and not very rewarding as a lot of

Tables neatly laid out for a Sunday school celebration tea in the Market Hall behind the Town Hall, probably in the 1920s

the children would leave Sunday school and go on to the parish church as they grew older, with that arrogance of feeling too big for the little chapel.

Mr Adams was a market gardener living by Eye Station, a very quietly spoken gentleman; no doubt he was taken advantage of by some of the children. Mr Tomlins was a railway signalman at Berrington and Eye Station, and later the Kington Junction Crossing in Mill Street, Leominster and he was also a JP at Leominster Magistrates Court. He was another very gentle man, but with more authority and firmer with the children. He could also play the harmonium and was a local preacher. His family, son Ira and daughters Olive and Gwen, were a great help in the Sunday school anniversaries, a little before my time in the Sunday school – about 1928 to 1930. Easter Sunday was memorable for the Easter egg and large Jaffa orange each, a gift from Mrs Bufton and carried on by her daughter, Mrs Apperley of Luston Bury Farm.

Herbert Millichamp

Even at my tender age I thought there couldn't be a more boring place on a wet Sunday afternoon in the winter than Leominster. Nothing was open, the town was dead and there was nowhere to go – except Sunday school!

After a morning of attending the service at the Priory Church, reading the Sunday papers and keeping the fire stacked up in the living room so that my father could cook the Sunday roast in the oven attached to the fire, along with everyone else in my family I sat down for dinner. This was the best meal of the week and always included meat, together with vegetables from the garden and roast potatoes. It was the only time that we ever had roast potatoes and oh, how we all looked forward to them.

After this major event was over and we had washed up the dishes, I walked with all my sisters to the chapel in Green Lane and spent the rest of the afternoon listening to Methodist fire and brimstone. Returning home for a quick tea, I was then packed off again to the Priory Church for the evening service, so I certainly got plenty of religion.

Roy Gough

Youth Organisations and Movements

In 1935 or 1936 I joined the British Red Cross, VAD (Voluntary Aid Detachment) in Leominster, and I'd go to meetings in the summer. There was a little bit of drill, so that you could take part

Inspecting the VAD detachment at the Grange, 1937

in the town parades and things like that. First Aid, home nursing, I got certificates for those. That was my first uniform. I've still got photographs of it. Blue: pantaloons and puttees. Of course we had to hand it in when we left.

I have some very pleasant memories, especially of a day's outing with the detachment to Liverpool and Birkenhead. I forget whether we went by ferry down the Mersey and back by tunnel or the other way round – because the new Mersey Tunnel had just opened at that time.

Herbert Millichamp

A year before the war broke out my father joined what was called the Voluntary Aid Detachment, to carry out first aid in the event of bombing. As a Christian, if he had been conscripted he would have expressed a wish to be a non-combatant. He took the training very seriously, and all through the war years he was regularly on duty in the event of emergencies.

Mervyn Bufton

The scoutmaster was a chap called Mr Carter, and he lived in a house next to the Baptist Church on Etnam Street. It was a nice old black and white place too [see photograph opposite], but it's been knocked down. He was a monumental mason and had a place down Pinsley Road, and the scout hut was down there too. Scout Hall we used to call it. Just a corrugated tin place, it seemed quite big to me then when I was smaller ... it was no great shakes, but it gave the Scouts somewhere to meet.

I think we met on a Thursday night. There were quite a few scouts, and we had patrols: the wood pigeon patrol, the peewits

Etnam Street with Mr Carter's black and white house on the right

and the owl patrol. The Cubs met there as well, Cubs and Guides. We used to go camping. I can remember going to Wales and we went up at Dinmore and a place called Kinsham. Presteigne, Eyton, we went all over the place. Get the tents out and off we'd go.

Ray Fisher

There was a club that the Methodists ran called the Girls Life Brigade. We had a uniform like the Girl Guides, and we learnt to do sewing and knitting, which was very good and gave us something to do. We met a couple of evenings a week after school, and we marched through the town on Remembrance Day. It was run by Miss Ragsdale. (She married Norman Davies, the chemist.) She organised the Brigade, and kept it going for a long, long time. Then it just gradually went.

Dorothy Oughton

There used to be sixpenny dances at the girls' club in Etnam Street, but I never went to them much. Miss Winterbourne used to run them. Miss Wintryfeet, the kids used to call her! She was a neighbour of ours for years. At Christmas she used to bring us a teapot and a quarter of tea, and she used to make her own toffee. I couldn't eat it, but the kids used to.

One of the girls was married to Frank Dale; she was a lovely piano player. She used to play the piano in her brother Cyril's band: the Cyril Morris Dance Band. My brother was in it too; he used to play the cornet. If anybody wanted some music for a dance they would go. They did well. My brother used to play the Last Post.

My dad played the big bass, and he and my brother were in Leominster Town Band.

Margery Hunt

Of course we had the Jubilee, about 1935, wasn't it? I was six or seven and there was a carnival, and they put me in a kilt. My parents got in touch with relatives in Scotland and they sent me a full ruddy outfit. I always remember that. It was a hot day. I didn't like it; I didn't like it at all!

There was something special for the kids. I'm not sure, but I think we went to Batemans Buildings or something like that, and they had trestle tables there and we all had jelly and ice cream.

John Sharp

Procession of children to the New Exchange Building as part of the celebrations of the Silver Jubilee of George V, May 1935

Entertainment and sport

The Wireless

There was great excitement every weekday night at a quarter to seven when the fifteen minute episode of 'Dick Barton, Special Agent' came on the wireless. Everything stopped for me at that time and I was glued to the set, sharing in the adventures of Dick, Jock and Snowy. However, my mother wasn't too impressed with any of these wonders, as while I was sharing their adventures I was oblivious to all else around me and wouldn't hear any entreaties to help with the younger children or other household tasks.

Roy Gough

The wireless started to get about, and you had an accumulator. Somebody gave my dad a little one, and I used to have to take it up the gas works to be charged, leave it there overnight then fetch it the next day, and they would charge you sixpence for that.

Margery Hunt

Oh, the radio! If you went in any of my aunts' houses after seven o'clock, it was 'Dick Barton Special Agent', and you dared not speak! It was absolute shhh! There was a garage opposite, Scandret's Garage, and we used to take the accumulator in, and he would put it on charge; it took about twenty-four hours to charge up. I think my aunt had a spare one – a huge great thing.

Pauline Davies

I worked at Scandret's at about the time I came out of the Army. My wife's parents had an accumulator. Hydrochloric acid, I think. If you dropped a spot on your clothes, it burned immediately. I know when I worked as a motor mechanic we did this charging and oh, my overalls, they'd be all ripped down. People would bring in their discharged batteries to be charged up, especially the country people on a Friday. Then they would pick their spare one up. Later there came the dry battery, which was much better. It still had to be charged, but you didn't have the problem of the acid falling on the furniture or on your clothes.

Alec Haines

We liked to listen on a Sunday night to the Ovaltineys on the radio. We took the accumulator to the shop down North Road and have it charged up. When we moved we'd take it to Downs' Garage in South Street, bring back the other one and keep on doing it that way. Mum liked to listen to the Archers but I liked the Ovaltineys.

We joined the Ovaltineys Club, and you had a badge which came through the post. Oh, you thought you were the world! – a gold badge because you'd been in it for so long. It seems laughable now, and children today wouldn't appreciate it, but it was marvellous to listen to the Ovaltineys.

Dorothy Oughton

The Cinema

We had a cinema in the Square – that brick building opposite Woolworth's [now closed]. It had beautiful stonework; there were offices all round the bow part and at one time it could hold seven hundred and fifty people. These people travelled round the county, putting on plays. I didn't see silent films; they were a thing of the past.

If you went into the cinema on your own, you always came out with company, that's what we used to say – because you were covered in fleas. We called that cinema the flea pit.

There was a chap who was in charge of us going in, a real old army sergeant major. We played all kinds of tricks on him. Because the toilet window was the other side of the building we used to get in through there for nothing.

Alec Haines

Once a month on a Saturday morning we were allowed to go to the matinée, me and my next brother, to the cinema in the square. It was four pence to go in. Mother somehow scraped up two fourpences and two ha'pennys, a ha'penny each for five toffees or a bit of liquorice, and that was our treat once a month. That was it, even if there was a good cowboy film on next week – sorry, there wasn't the money to do it.

Malcolm Newman

The picture house I knew was in the Corn Square. I think I had about a shilling pocket money, and I liked to use it to go to the pictures. It wasn't very dear, but if you went up in the nice seats at

Corn Square and the Corn Exchange Building in the 1950s

the back, you had to pay more. If you went down in the front it was about sixpence. My sister-in-law was the cashier there. Mr Benson used to run it. They had music – his daughter played a pianola, music on a roll of paper, and somebody used to play a violin.

Margery Hunt

At the cinema in Corn Square, it was tuppence to go downstairs and fourpence to go up. We could only afford tuppence, but my auntie was the usherette there and sometimes she let us go upstairs. We though we were the cat's whiskers then. Whenever we had tuppence we would go to the pictures. We couldn't go in free because she was only the usherette; she wasn't in the box office. Then they opened the other one; that was six pence downstairs and a shilling to go upstairs, which was a lot of money then. They kept that one open in the square for a bit, and then it started to dwindle because they had better films in the other one.

If there was a colour film, it was called Technicolour then, and there used to be queues and queues to go to one of those, because it was pretty – colours and all that – something out of the ordinary after black and white.

Dorothy Oughton

Usually on a Sunday night it was a cowboy film, and there would be a queue that went round into Westbury Street. It was amazing really. I think there was one film on Monday, Tuesday and Wednesday and another on Thursday, Friday and Saturday. Saturday morning you had children's films. They were great; I think it only cost about sixpence to go in. Your mum and dad would give you the money to go, just to get you out of the way.

Ray Fisher

The only entertainment for us children was Saturday morning cinema. We had the Saturday morning club. Of course it was all cinema then. Everybody went to the cinema. As far as entertainment is concerned that was about all there was in Leominster at that time.

The Clifton cinema opened on the day that I was born. My Uncle Bert had the first ticket, and he always carried it in his

An advert for the Leominster Picture Palace in the Corn Exchange in 1913 proudly included this picture of the interior. The Leominster News *carried the advert for the cinema on its front page for many years, and in 1936 started a four page Leominster Picture News supplement for the picturegoers of the town*

LEOMINSTER AMUSEMENTS

CLIFTON CINEMA, SUNDAY NEXT, APRIL 2nd, at 8.15. Doors open at 7.45.

BOBBY BREEN and BASIL RATHBONE in MAKE A WISH

Also GENE AUTRY in BOOTS AND SADDLES U

CLIFTON CINEMA

MONDAY, APRIL 3rd.   FOR 3 DAYS

RAYMOND MASSEY
in
BLACK LIMELIGHT A

Also NEIL HAMILTON in
HOLLYWOOD STADIUM MYSTERY A

THURSDAY, APRIL 6th.   FOR 2 DAYS ONLY
(No Performance Good Friday)

The Film you have been waiting for.

SABU
of "Elephant Boy" fame, in
THE DRUM U

(In Gorgeous Technicolour)

PICTURE HOUSE

MONDAY, APRIL 3rd.   FOR 3 DAYS

JOHN BARRYMORE
in
BULLDOG DRUMMOND'S PERIL U

ALSO
Bob Burns in ARKANSAS TRAVELLER U

THURSDAY, APRIL 6th.   FOR 2 DAYS ONLY
(No Performance Good Friday)

CAROLE LOMBARD & FREDERIC MARCH
in
NOTHING SACRED A

In Gorgeous Technicolour.
ALSO
Richard Talmadge in SPEED REPORTER A

The Clifton cinema and the Picture House were showing the latest releases in Gorgeous Technicolour in April 1939

wallet. In those days they had a commissionaire, all dressed up, on the door. He was very strict, and we weren't allowed in unless it was a 'B' film, which was the Disney kind of film. If there was an 'A' film – horror films and things like that – we had to have someone to take us in if we were, say, over ten. We used to pester our aunties to give them the money, or they wouldn't let us in.

Pauline Davies

We did go to the cinema occasionally. The first film Judith and I ever saw was 'Snow White and the Seven Dwarves'. I loved it, but Judith howled her head off because she was frightened of the witch, and she had to be taken out.

Maureen Crumpler

The most wonderful place in the town, even more attractive than all the churches and chapels, was the cinema. On Saturday mornings, provided I had earned the few pennies necessary for admittance, I could enter this magnificent building controlled by a giant in a spectacular commissionaire's uniform, and worship at the altar of celluloid. With all the boys of the town I could join in the gunfights with Jean Autry or Roy Rogers and cause mayhem for the girls, or sit in boredom while the girls wept during the adventures of Lassie or Shirley Temple. Oh, I loved those Saturday mornings – they made up for all the troubles of the week.

Roy Gough

The Grange

The Grange was a natural meeting place for the town. There was cricket almost every day, nothing better. There was a Thursday afternoon match, and one on Saturday afternoon, and then on Mondays, Wednesdays and Fridays there was knock-out cricket. The semi-finals and finals would draw 200 people. Yes, it was a prime feature of Leominster life.

Mervyn Bufton

We had a first and second team; two teams from Leominster, two teams from Bromyard, one from Tenbury, one from the Luctonians, and a team from Kington. We had knock-outs of 18 overs. Especially on a Friday, you would have people coming who had come in from the country to go to the market. There were seats on the banks, but people would be all the way round, you had to be there before six o'clock for a 6.30 start.

Alec Haines

We were watching a knock-out cricket match at the Grange one night. Now, Mr Peatt the vet used to keep a few horses. I don't know what happened quite, but this horse got away from Fred Pilliner, who worked for Mr Peatt, and he came up the road round the Grange, and went galloping through and this chap, I can see him now, he was on his pushbike after him. He didn't catch him! The horse went down Church Street and got so far up High Street and then he crashed into Hunters the grocer's window. He smashed the window and was killed.

Fred Parsons

They'd get hundreds of people watching the knock-out cricket matches on the Grange. The Blue Boar, the Old and Bold, the farmers from Stoke Prior, the Broad Ramblers, they all had teams in the knock-out. People used to flock in to watch.

It was all right until somebody wanted to walk across the path. They had to stop the game while some little old lady decided she wanted to walk across, and she'd go trundling across there with her walking stick.

There weren't so many things to do in those days so you made the most of what you could do. We used to go down to the Grange and play cricket and football. We used the Grange in those days a hundred times more than they do today. Kids were always there on a Saturday morning. They used to organise games between themselves – South Street against the Crescent and that type of thing. To play cricket you needed a bat, a ball and a tree. If you

The pavilion on the Grange

wanted to play football you put your coats down for the goalposts. When we used to go hop picking with our parents they might buy us a football; so in the hop picking season you'd go down the Grange and there'd be five or six footballs being kicked about.

Ray Fisher

Because the junior school didn't have any playing field, they used to play on the Grange. The Lower Grange, where all the slides and things are now, used to be a little football pitch, and we had our six-a-side league there. We had eight or nine teams from the school, and they played six-a-side football every night after school in the football season. The other part of the Grange was the cricket pitch. On a Sunday morning, all the lads used to go down there and we'd have a forty-a-side football game, coats down to make the goal posts, right outside Grange Court.

But cricket was a big thing in Leominster. Many a night when I was a tiddler, it would be nothing to have five or six hundred people in the Grange watching the cricket.

Tony Rock

There used to be boxing in Leominster. They held boxing contests in Yeomans Yard in Westbury Street. Westbury Street was completely different then to what it is now. Little tiny street it was. Morgans used to have their livestock lorries from the market, because they lived right by there. Dishley Street was a tiny street then too, when the market was there. Every so often they'd have a boxing ring in there, and local people from all around would box. They had them down at the very bottom of Etnam Street as well. Right by the White Lion, there used to be a place called Sharps

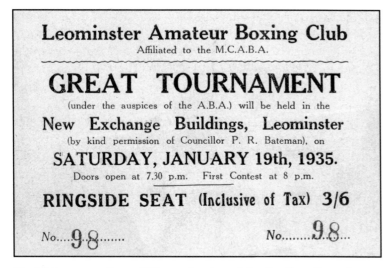

Leominster Amateur Boxing Club

Affiliated to the M.C.A.B.A.

GREAT TOURNAMENT

(under the auspices of the A.B.A.) will be held in the

New Exchange Buildings, Leominster

(by kind permission of Councillor P. R. Bateman), on

SATURDAY, JANUARY 19th, 1935.

Doors open at 7.30 p.m.   First Contest at 8 p.m.

RINGSIDE SEAT (Inclusive of Tax) 3/6

No....98........   No.........98....

Yard. They were from different boxing clubs, Ludlow, Leominster, Hereford places like that.

Ray Fisher

The old boss liked a bet, but in those days it wasn't legal to go to a betting shop. There was none of that. He used to get a chap to call every day to take his bet.

Fred Parsons

My dad loved to do the horses. Thruppence each way, that was the limit. If he won anything, he would put it up; he was ever such a saver. The bookie was Birdy Morris. He was a painter and decorator who lived in Mill Street, and he used to take in bets. I took them down to his house more than once. He had two daughters, he'd be at work, and they'd take them in for him. They reckoned these girls used to open them, and if they reckoned the horse wasn't going to win they'd stand it. But one day, this one horse surprised them and came in first, and they didn't know what to do! They knew they'd get into trouble off their dad, so their mother covered up for them and put the money in.

Margery Hunt

Health and safety

I came home one day and said to Mother, 'Archie's not very well today, Mam.' She said, 'He'll have to put up with it. Your father is off getting work, there's no money coming in, and he'll have to put up with it!' That's all you'd have. We owed the doctor's for ever more, a few bob or whatever it was. Mother used to struggle to try and pay for it. I know it wasn't much, but it was a few shillings, wasn't it? When you were working on the farm, if you fell ill, it was your bad luck. They couldn't do much about it; you had to hope for the best.

Arthur Edwards

I was in hospital for a couple of days after an accident, and then I came out and my father used to carry me from North Road up to Dr Kingdom. He would carry me up on his back every day. At the end of Broad Street, on the right hand side, that's was where the doctor was.

Dorothy Oughton

Our doctor was Dr Kingdom, and his surgery was as you went down Broad Street, right on the bend that goes into New Street. I can remember his surgery, and the hard chairs in the waiting room. It wasn't nice and plush like these places are now. Of course if your sister or your brother had chickenpox then we were all put in together and we all got it. We had measles, German measles and chickenpox, mumps, all those kind of things. Doctors would come and visit you at a minute's notice in those days. Dr Kingdom was such a kind person. He spoke to you in a very slow, quiet voice: 'How are you feeling today?' Dr Kingdom ... good name, that.

Ray Fisher

You would have to be very bad to get the doctor. He would be most people's last call, because they couldn't afford the bills. When I was a kid we had a Dr Steele, and he lived in Church Street; Dr Thompson went in with him. As a young man Dr Thompson used to ride a motor bike on his rounds. You'd hear him coming on this motor bike. He was a proper dappy little man, but he was a nice doctor, very gentlemanly. Dr Steele was a big man, and he wore a trench coat and a flat cap, and alloy glasses. We'd had the measles, and of course you had to report it then. You had to have the doctor, and he came and told our mam what to do.

Elwood's the chemist was in Drapers Lane. When one of us was poorly or had a cough, Mum used to tell me to fetch me six pennyworth of raspberry vinegar and olive oil, and Mr Elwood used to make it up. It was only a little bottle, three inches high. My mum used to give me a little drop on a spoon.

Margery Hunt

In those days my parents contributed to the Midland Mutual Aid Benefit Society, something of that order, which obviously was a great help when it came to meeting the doctor's bills. I can remember going to the doctor's consulting room at the bottom of Broad Street on a Friday, and he told me to go to bed straight away. Well, I went to bed and I think I had a Rupert book with me, but by the end of the day I must have been feeling not at all good, and I've no recollection of anything that happened after that until the following Friday. There were no antibiotics in 1938 (or was it 1939?). It would be interesting to know what medicine I was given, apart from slices of orange.

Mervyn Bufton

I took my little girl to the gas works for whooping cough but it didn't seem to do her much good. Then they'd say that to help them with breathing you should take them first thing in the morning into a flock of sheep. I don't know ... some old wives' tales. There used to be a thing ... I don't know what they called ... a shamrock or summat; it used to grow on the roofs. If you had an abscess on your neck, they used to say, 'Get one of those, warm it and put it on your neck, and it'll break the abscess.' When my mum had a whitlow and she couldn't get rid of it, this old lady told her to get some shamrock, and she warmed it and tied it round my mum's finger.

Margery Hunt

The women did have a hard time. They had hair buns at the back and little pinafores and at forty they were finished, really. Through hard work they looked like seventy-year-olds look now. They weren't worried about themselves and their appearance; they were worried about making a living and bringing up their children.

Leominster was always a very superstitious town, especially the women. If there was a hole in a loaf of bread someone was going to die. If there was a spider on the wall something terrible was going to happen. Someone was going to die; someone was going to get killed. Oh yes, we had all that.

Pauline Davies

"Leominster was always a very superstitious town."

Another superstition was that when there was a thunderstorm, you had to turn your mirror and all your pictures round, so the lightning wouldn't strike the window. Oh, you couldn't have a mirror showing.

Dorothy Oughton

There was a dentist, Mr Lewis, in a place called the Lighthouse. (It was called that because there was a stained glass window on the door with a lighthouse in it.) My grandmother took me there when the enamel started to come off my teeth. I don't know why, because we didn't have a lot of sweets. When she saw the dentist she said, 'I want you to take this girl's teeth out, and if you won't do it I'll take her to somebody who will.'

I'd have been fourteen or fifteen then, working at the *Leominster News* office. With the needle, I had all my top teeth taken out, and half the bottom, in a week. It was just one of those things. She said it and that was it. It happened whether you liked it or not.

Minnie Davies

The school dentist, God, they were terrible! All the kids were coming out 'mmmmmm', with handkerchiefs and blood running down. They used to pull them out, didn't they? He'd have a field day! And the nit nurse used to come round to look at your hair to see if you'd got any nits. What a job that was! They'd lift your hair up and have a look. You could see the kids who had nits because they'd say, 'Go and stand over there!' I found out years later that nits wouldn't go into dirty hair.

Ray Fisher

My Uncle Tommy, who used to deliver at the International, used to tell me tales. He said he never went to the dentist. He used to go to the Talbot and there was a chap in there who was a dentist, and Tommy'd buy him a whisky to pull his teeth out.

Denise Pugh

My father's shop in South Street had a front shop where they sold toothpaste and cigarettes and hair cream … Brylcreem was the thing. Through the shop and on the upstairs landing, a dentist rented the one room and the next room was a ladies' hairdressers.

The dentist's chair when we were kids was one of the old-fashioned ones, you could turn the handle and lean back. He had a drill with a sort of treadmill that turned the thing, and he drilled your teeth. Downstairs there was a waiting room, and there was a phone in there. If ever the phone rang my dad or my mum had to answer it. We never answered the phone, it was far too important!

Ray Fisher

There was always a policeman around; they had their regular beat. I remember once my brother was misbehaving in the High Street. PC Bowrey lived on the Bargates, and he came around the corner, looked down at my brother and just moved him on with a motion of the eyes …

Mervyn Bufton

You weren't allowed to play football in the street then. My brother and his mates were kicking a ball about when PC Rees came along. They ran him all the way to Broadwood. They couldn't run any more, and he was done up himself, from running after them. They used to get on well with him, but they used to tease him a lot.

Inspector Edge lived in Bridge Street. He was a tall man, with dark hair and a dark moustache, and when I was a kid if I saw

A policeman on point duty at the Iron Cross in front of Seager & Sons, Fish and Fruit Merchants, in about 1940

him coming I used to tremble. I was frightened to death of him. All the kids were. Many a time we've been coming home from school the Mill Head way as we used to call it, down past the Priory and over the bridge, and if he came towards us in Mill Street, we were that frightened we'd run all the way back and down the town.

Margery Hunt

When Dad was on the delivery van, he used to stop near Alton. He'd been up and got the lady's orders, and he'd been given half a dozen eggs in an old-fashioned blue sugar bag. He came down to the van and there was a policeman walking his beat. He looked at Dad – he knew him of course – and he poked his walking stick straight into this bag of eggs. Broke the lot. Anyway, Dad got the policeman to pay him for the eggs, and then he ate them!

Minnie Davies

Oh, the police were very severe. If you were two boys talking, the policeman'd move you on, and give you a kick up the bum as well! Children were terrified of the police. You couldn't regard them as friends. They were from the Victorian period, really, and they weren't very well educated, let's be honest. There was some local crime, mainly trivial things, breaking a window or something like that. There wasn't much drunkenness, but there were three notable families in Leominster who always wanted to have a fight.

There was a policeman on duty at night on West Street off the Iron Cross, but you wouldn't see him! The bakehouse was going all night, and he'd be in there having food and cups of tea. The police gained a lot of information from local people, you know, if something was not quite right.

Alec Haines

There used to be two policemen on duty at night. One used to go one way, and one the other, then the bakers would come on duty about 3 o'clock in the morning, and the policemen would have a cup of tea in the baker's shop!

On busy days, one policeman used to be on point duty at the Iron Cross. PC Thomas used to get a bit ratty there – 'You silly B's!' he used to shout.

Fred Parsons

One thing that particularly sticks in my memory about the Iron Cross is that there was always a policeman standing on the pavement and looking straight up West Street. He was always a big policeman too! Resplendent in his dark uniform with shiny buttons and a large helmet, he was the embodiment of authority to me, and when walking past him, I always passed behind his back, hoping he wouldn't notice me and challenge me about some of the escapades I had been up to!

Roy Gough

On a Friday, they used to have a policeman on the Iron Cross on point duty. But not always! My dad used to have a chair in the front shop, and very often the policeman would be sitting in there, having a chat, seeing what was going on. I suppose he would nip out if there was a commotion.

Ray Fisher

PC Bull lived up Church Street; the police houses were two houses next to the big house. The police knew how to deal with things. I didn't mind him clipping my ear, as long as he didn't tell my mother! I was petrified of that. The courts had nothing to do with it, and you didn't get a criminal record. I just find all of this fascinating, the way people dealt with each other.

Denise Pugh

Jack and Peggy Peatt, they were nice people, and they had these delicious peach trees. There were lovely peaches hanging over the wall that goes up Churchill Avenue. But the local bobby, Mr Wallace, told us 'Don't touch 'em' and that was enough. You didn't touch them because the policeman had told you not to.

Tony Rock

Once there was a new police inspector going round at night, when he first arrived here. When his driver was going to drive straight past a certain pub, he told the driver to stop outside. He insisted on going into the pub, and the result was that all the local gossip which the police used to get through this pub ceased. The main source of criminal information dried up. That caused a little bit of a to-do.

Denis Turton

Getting about

Everything went up and down the High Street, and often two vehicles would get stuck. The Midland Red buses used to go into the square, through Corn Street, and out the other side by Smith and Son the paper shop. To get out of there they used to get right up on the pavement and just miss the building. People had to get out of the way.

Fred Parsons

I used to use Bengry's bus backwards and forwards between Kington and Leominster. It didn't take very long, and it was quite exciting. It was always packed; you couldn't get a seat unless you got on in Kington. By the time we got to Leominster they were standing up squashed in the aisle.

Daphne Mayall

We didn't have a car, but my father was always very insistent that every year we always went away for a holiday, preferably to the coast. He said it was very important to get away, so for two weeks we had a holiday. I've got happy memories of those holidays. Sometimes we went to the seaside in Pembrokeshire, other times we went to Aberystwyth, where we used to have caravan holidays. I remember we went down to the Mumbles, down beyond Swansea. The train service was the main means of transport in those days, of course – there were lots of branch lines. Coaches weren't so frequent, everybody used the train service.

Before the war people didn't travel much. If somebody went abroad, boy! You'd think they'd gone to the end of the earth. It was unheard of. If somebody had crossed the Channel to France you looked at them almost in amazement.

Doug Lewis

My dad worked on the road gang. He used his bike for work, sometimes he was at Kingsland or sometimes Kington, according to where they were working. They had to make their own way there.

They had liquid tar in a big vat. It was warmed up, put into this big sprayer with holes in, and sprayed over, then they'd put the gravel across the road and steam roller it. They'd throw one skimming on and roll it, then they'd put another skimming on and roll it again. Everybody wanted to see the steam roller going. It was something different, wasn't it? They never had much protective clothing on. Dad used to come home sometimes covered in tar and he had to get it off outside – he spoilt a lot of clothes doing that. But they were good roads.

Dorothy Oughton

It was really exciting when the road repair gang came along the road. The gang centred on a huge steamroller that clanked along at about two miles per hour with bursts of steam and a piercing whistle. It smelt strongly of coal and sweet-smelling tar. Behind the steam roller and pulled by it was a cart filled with coal for the boilers, another filled with water, and another filled with chippings and tar for repairing the roads, and behind that came the caravan home of the driver. He was a little red-faced man dressed in greasy black overalls and a greasy black cap, and we envied the life of romance he led, travelling the open roads.

He used to come past the big horses outside the blacksmith's shop. Just passing the horses with his steam roller was trouble enough as they would fret and rear with fear, but when the little man stopped at the Bowling Green Pub for a quick pint of cider,

Resurfacing West Street in the mid 1930s. The stone is carried by horse-drawn cart and wheelbarrows to create a new surface which is finished by a steamroller

the prolonged hissing of steam and shrilling of the whistle would send the horses mad with fear, and their handlers would have the greatest difficulty controlling them. My, we did find it fun to watch!

Roy Gough

"The hissing of steam would send the horses mad with fear."

I'd lived within sight of the railway, and the trains were running back and fore less than a mile away, but I never went in a train until I was 18. I went from Leominster to Hereford, and then I was put on a train from Hereford to go across London to Caterham, in Surrey. That was my first long journey. Nervous, we would stop at every station, and I was writing down their names as we passed.

Herbert Millichamp

My father used to catch the train; I think it was commonly known as the Kington Coffee Pot, because it had a long funnel. He'd come down every weekend, from Birmingham to Worcester, and then at Worcester he'd change for Leominster. It was the very last train down, so it stopped at every station and every halt on the way. There was a little gaslight at each station, which was the only light allowed, apparently, and the guard got out at each one and turned the light off.

Maureen Crumpler

Leominster railway station was very much used. We had five railway lines, and then you had the lines for all the cattle and sheep and horses. We had a restaurant on number one platform, and on the middle lodge there was a signal box. The trains would depart for Kingsland, Kington and New Radnor. Then there was

Leominster station as it was in 1910;
the photograph shows all five platforms

another line that went up the other way and branched up to Brimfield, for Worcester and on to London. We lost all that.

During the war they had one called the 'Bomber' – it was more like a vehicle than a train, and it took all the workers from Shrewsbury, picked up here at Leominster, and went on to the ammunition factory at Rotherwas in Hereford.

Alec Haines

"You wouldn't need an alarm clock. You would hear the train."

You wouldn't need an alarm clock. You would hear the train. We always went by the train, the Mail going through in the mornings. It went up to Kington at six o'clock, then back down. My brother-in-law was a signal man on the train. He used to peep his horn when he was on, to tell me it was time to get up.

There was a man who lived at the railway house, and he used to open the gates. There's many a time he overslept and we heard such a crash, and they'd gone through ... Oh yes, the gates smashed, the train driver couldn't stop as he came round the corner from the station, and he'd just built up steam. The crossing gate keeper used to get in the Prince of Wales in Bridge Street, have a drink and forget to open the gates. More than once the train was coming round, and my husband and another chap rushed and got them open. Poor old Ernie would come struggling down, and he'd say 'It ent that time, is it?'

Margery Hunt

Food and shopping

Until recent years the main local shops were owner-occupied and in many cases the owners lived over the shops: Ross the shoe maker in High Street, Fosters on the corner of Rainbow Street, Normans the newsagent. The optician in the town was also the jeweller, Reg Mayall. Norman Davies was the chemist in Corn Square. Mrs Newey ran a very high class dress shop on the corner of School Lane. Gradually they all moved out.

Denis Turton

We used to have our bread from Pewtress' bakehouse and shop at the bottom of Broad Street. He made the most beautiful Chelsea buns and doughnuts you could ever taste. He used to make them on a Thursday night, and sell them on a Friday. My brother and I would call there on our way to Bargates School. Mum would give us a bag and a penny to buy a Chelsea bun, which Mr Pewtress cut in two for our lunch. They were so big you couldn't eat one on your own. It was our Friday treat. My brother would eat his before he got to school!

Then there was Fletchers. Old Barclay started it all off, made thousands. He lived in Broad Street, and he was agent for all the papers. You'd see the boys on a Sunday, going on their bikes, delivering the papers out to the country. His own children did it too, but he paid them no more than the others. He also made money from rags and bones. He would take your rabbit skins and if they were in good condition he'd give you a penny, but if they weren't it'd be a ha'penny. Barclay opened a butcher's shop on one side of the passage for his son, and a sweet shop on the other side for his daughter. His eldest son, Jack, was a good butcher. He used to breed his own cows and sheep, and they used to slaughter them. Their meat was beautiful, Fletchers Meat.

Where we lived in Bridge Street we had a little shop each side of us. They sold everything – a cut of bacon (it wasn't packed in those days), or a rabbit. There were dealers in second-hand clothes too. One of them had a coat, I tried it on and it was beautiful. She wanted four shillings for it. My mum gave me two shillings towards it, and the woman in the shop kept the coat until I had the other two shillings. She wouldn't let me have it and owe her.

There was a clothing shop where Longley's is, she had coats and frocks and that. If you wanted one, you gave her your shilling a week until it was paid for. You wouldn't hear of a young girl getting in debt like they do today. Thorns the boot shop; they were just above the Central. He started up a shoe club. You could get a pair of shoes, but you couldn't have them till you paid for them!

Margery Hunt

BROAD STREET, LEOMINSTER

20607

Photograph of Broad Street in the late 1940s

My husband had Mayall the Jewellers. He was an optician, and his parents used to run the jewellery shop. Eventually we sold the rest of it and ended up with just the optician's. My grandparents were 'Blomers' who had the chemist's in Broad Street. My grandfather worked in the shop – he died fairly early on, but I remember he was a great big man, very tall. I used to go and stay with my grandparents quite a bit, I used to love it. The shop front is still there. Sometimes when the side doors are open, and they're rather beautiful doors, I can look up the path into the garden where the pond and lawn were and it brings it all back. My mother was born there.

Daphne Mayall

Bach's shop in the High Street
with delivery vans parked outside

The High Street was full of shops. There was Burtons the grocers, Maypole, Home and Colonial, International, Guy Smith, Jack Bach on the other side, general grocer. Berrington Hall dealt quite a lot with Bach's, he was a bit higher class, as he sold wines and spirits and all that. Friday was the shopping day. People used to come in on buses and trains. Most of the shops had a van which delivered orders round to all the different places.

Fred Parsons

My mum used to go to International for her shopping. You went in through the door and on the left, that's where you asked for all your groceries. They had a chair, and my mother would sit

High Street from the Iron Cross

there and give her list in. There were two shop assistants. There was another counter where you could get cheese, butter and all that, and sometimes the assistants knew what Mum wanted and they would go and get the stuff from that side. Mr Andrews was the manager. My brother went to work there for a bit when he left school. He did some work inside, but mainly he delivered groceries. He had a bike with one of those big baskets on the front. At the weekend there were some from out in the country that wanted their groceries, but he couldn't do it all on the bike, so they had a van to take some out into the country.

It was lovely, International, it was very, very friendly. Burtons was quite nice, too – it was bigger, and had a double-fronted window, and they sold more or less the same things, but my mother found that International was friendly and helpful, so that's where she went.

Woodwards had a little shop up West Street, and there was Melias, Burtons – so many little shops like that. I loved going into them and being served individually. You were treated as an individual.

Dorothy Oughton

Above: International Stores in the 1930s

International Stores advert, 1939

Dad had a good job, and my mum was pretty good at cooking. She bought a joint every Saturday. Yapp and Powells was the butchers then, in the High Street. They'd deliver the joint on a Saturday and my mum would roast it. We used to love the lovely roast dinner on a Sunday, and then she'd make a bit of a stew. We had good food, I can't say I ever went hungry. I went more hungry in the war when I was married than I did when I was a kid.

Margery Hunt

Mother didn't go to the shops every day. She used to make her own bread, and make soups with vegetables. She would even boil the bones so that the goodness came out, and make broth. It was on the stove practically every day. We enjoyed it. Sunday dinner was a rabbit. Mum used to skin it, sew the tummy up with some stuffing, and roast it. We would have a big Yorkshire pudding cut up into slices, and a nice big rice pudding or something like that for afters. Dad was quite good in the garden; he liked to grow his own vegetables, so we weren't too bad in that respect. And when he was on the Council some of the farmers used to let him have a swede. We were lucky.

Dorothy Oughton

I used to love chitterlings. We bought them off the butcher. Well, he was retired, but he used to go about helping to kill pigs, and he got the chitterlings. His wife would boil them, and I kept the twisted ones. I ate them cold with salt and mustard. Once you tasted them, you loved them. What else did we have? Cow's udder, absolutely lovely. You roasted it with onions, and it was

just like chicken. Different things we had in those days, things people wouldn't look at now. The grocer would have some scraps of bacon for sixpence, and we'd fry it up. We didn't have bacon very often because we couldn't afford it.

When I got the fire going, the kids would scrub up a potato, dry them and put one each in the oven before they went to school, and have them for their tea. They loved them.

Margery Hunt

"Cow's udder, absolutely lovely ..."

Some things were delivered to the door: bread and milk, and the Kleeneze man would come along perhaps once every three months with his suitcase full of wax polish and brushes and brooms. There were certain shops which attracted attention. Taylor and Ward's on the High Street was a fascinating shop, with all the nuts and bolts, and nails and screws, and tools.

Mervyn Bufton

We used to call Page's in School Lane the Sixpenny Bazaar. My mum could remember it opening. When they opened it on a Saturday, Mrs Page said, 'Here goes! All I've got to our name is sixpence, but we've got a shop full.' They sold out within a few hours!

You name it, they sold it – they sold everything. They sold a lot of toys but nothing dear or big. They sold dishes, cups and saucers, basins, plates, brooms, brushes. I went down there to get my soap and washing powder. It was very cheap. They called it the Sixpenny Bazaar, and there was supposed to be nothing over sixpence, but if you went for a saucepan, it would be sixpence for the lid and sixpence for the saucepan. They had a club before Christmas; if we saw anything we wanted it was put by, but we couldn't have it till we paid for it.

The son, Billy, took it over. He told me about some of the artful kids who came in the shop. One girl would come in to do her mother's shopping, give him two bob, and then say she'd given him half a crown. That was a regular thing, till he checked on her, and found her out.

Margery Hunt

That shop where Parry's is now in the High Street used to be Palliser's. The windows were always open, and they used to have all the chickens and pheasants and things hanging down.

Dorothy Oughton

Charlie Harvey kept the men's shop. They had two shops in Corn Street, one either side of the street, and they sold shirts and underwear one side, suits on the other. He was a big boy at the Rankin Club, the Conservative Club, in the square. And there was Jack Bach, he kept Bach's, one of the posh grocers in the town, and a feller named Jack Rawlins, who was the salesman at Friars Garage, down South Street. People like that had the front room at the Conservative Club, It wasn't a written rule, but nobody else went in there, they sort of weren't allowed. Men like that weren't pint drinkers, you know, they used to drink what they called sticks. They were small glasses, not half a pint even.

They met occasionally at the Oak at Barons Cross. There was a gang of them who used to go in there and buy a round, you know. Anyway, this one chap, he was the local baker, just before it was his turn he would say: 'Well, I must go now'. There was another chap, Ben Davies, who farmed out at Hinton, and one morning he ordered double whiskies all round and said to the baker, 'It's your turn now!' They often told that story in the barber's shop.

Fred Parsons

When it was time to have one's first suit, that was quite something. Being of a poor family it was a long time before my brother and I got into long trousers, as they cost much more than shorts. I suppose I was about twelve when I was taken to Bradley's, at the Church Street end of Drapers Lane. I can remember that because my brother had a suit of the same cloth, but he had a double-breasted jacket and mine was single-breasted. We were happy to have a little bit of difference. It was off the peg. It was only towards my late teens that I went for made to measure, usually at Burtons in Hereford. They had a reputation for good cloth, and there was a Leominster man who managed it, so it was the right place to go.

Mervyn Bufton

DRAPERS LANE, LEOMINSTER

Near Bradley's the clothier, there used to be Bracknell's the fish and chip shop up in Drapers Lane. Oh, he used to do the most beautiful fish and chips. As young girls, we'd scrape together our money and go and sit in the little room in Bracknell's and share a pennorth of chips.

Margery Hunt

Mr Young was in School Lane, he was a boot repair man. Sometimes if it was a cold day we'd pop in for a chat, because it was always nice and warm in his shop. He'd be repairing the shoes and talking with a mouthful of nails. Opposite his shop was McEwan's the bakers. We used to call in there on our way down to the Grange, and buy a cake. Those were the days.

The Tudor Café was in the Square. The waitresses wore black and white, very smart. There was table cloths and little tables, and you wouldn't have a spoonful of sugar, you'd have a lump, and hold the cup in two fingers. Further up in Corn Street was Sid Wright's, W.H. Wright, greengrocers and fish merchants, and then there was Harvey's, the gents' outfitter. He had a shop on either side of the road, and Mr Carter would stand in the doorway with the tape measure round his neck, ready to measure you up.

Ray Fisher

I went to work at the *Leominster News* office on the corner of the Square and Drapers Lane, where the Tourist Information Centre is now. They sold newspapers, trinkets, Christmas cards, blotting paper, postcards of the town, and of course they printed the *Leominster News* there. Mr Baker was the manager and Miss

Watkins was the manageress of the shop. We weren't supposed to have a break in the morning, but Miss Watkins used to send one of us out with a paper or something we were supposed to exchange in Smiths or somewhere, and that was our excuse to go out and get half a pint of milk. Then we'd go down into the cellar where they'd got a little darkroom, a sort of little tunnel that went out under the Square. We had a jet so we could boil a kettle and

The Corn Square Pharmacy and the Tudor Café in the 1950s drawn by an anonymous artist

79

Left: Drapers Lane South. Right: The offices of the Leominster Printing Company and the Leominster News on the corner of Drapers Lane, with a model of the Ducking Stool above the door

make a cup of tea. I never knew why we weren't allowed lunch, but every morning I walked up to the top of Green Lane to fetch Mr Baker his basket with his Thermos and his lunch in.

I left the *Leominster News* to help my father with his business but I used to go back part time on a Thursday afternoon to get the paper ready for the post, and then I'd go in all day on a Friday to help with the market trade.

Minnie Davies

There used to be a family, the Watkins, they were the chimney sweeps. Every Thursday night they used to go and collect the *Leominster News*, and they used to deliver them down Bridge Street and right down to The Brode [The Broad].

Margery Hunt

Percy Briggs had a tiny watchmaker's shop in the High Street opposite Bright's the butcher's. He used to come on the bus every day. He was a well known chap; always had a nice big flower in his button hole. If you were late, they'd say, 'You're about as reliable as a Percy Briggs watch!' He was a great character. Every dinnertime he and his friends used to go and play crib in the Queen's Head – every dinnertime.

Ray Fisher

There were lots of shops either side of Drapers Lane, sweet shops and so on. There was one in particular, a tobacconist and sweet shop called Morrows. Bob Morrow; that was my favourite one. Another one was run by Mr Artois; he was a Frenchman and a barber, and he had a sweet shop in the front and his barber shop at the back, almost next to Morrows. There was a meat shop down

there, chap named Higgins. They used to sell sausage and cooked meats. I think they had a stall outside down there. At times Drapers Lane was full up with different stalls.

Fred Parsons

Friday was when all the country people came in to get their shopping from the grocer's for the week. They'd come in with their list, and the groceries were delivered by boys on a three-wheel bike with a basket on the front to a big room down there. Always whistling! They were always whistling, those boys! And then the people would come and collect them, and take their horse and trap or whatever it was home again.

Alec Haines

In the 1950s Saxby's was on the corner of South Street and West Street, by the Talbot. You could give him your list, you know, and ask him to deliver. He'd know what type of bacon you wanted,

Drapers Lane in the 1920s

what type of cheese, and so on. He'd put the order up, and there was a fellow called Jim Beard who delivered all the orders. You didn't have to wait or collect your own groceries.

Fred Parsons

Sometimes when we were wandering through the town looking for something to do and something to eat we would spot our big brother Dennis on his shop bicycle. Dennis was some years older than me. He had left school and in my eyes had a very important and exciting job. He was a delivery boy for a local grocery store owned by a man named Roughie Gough, who was no relation of ours. The bike Dennis rode with pride was a heavy and battered old one, with a basket on the front in which he carried the groceries to be delivered, and sometimes he would give us a ride.

The whole town was his oyster and he would ride all over it doing his duty, carefree, happy and proud of his responsibilities. Being that much older he tended to look down on us, but sometimes he would give us a couple of pennies from his tips and we would fill our tummies with teacakes.

Roy Gough

You could go into any men's hairdressers in Leominster and you only paid fourpence, but you were in a great big queue. Your hair had grown longer by the time you got to him!

Alec Haines

In the 1930s there were a lot of hairdressers in the town. There was Mr Hillman in the High Street, and Mr Lord down Etnam

Street. Our shop, Mr Fisher, was in Church Street. We left there in early spring of 1935 and moved to South Street, right opposite the back entrance to the Talbot.

When I started, a haircut was sixpence for men, fourpence for boys, and threepence for a shave. If the boys behaved themselves the boss used to give them a penny back, which meant threepence. We must have had about seventy old fellers who used to come for a shave. Some used to come every day, some perhaps twice a week, some once a week. To begin with I was just a lather boy; I'd put the lather on and then the boss used to come with the open razor and shave them. Eventually I could do the shaving myself. Shaving was a nuisance; it took longer to do a shave than it did to do a haircut, so it wasn't profitable really.

Fred Parsons

Harry Foster the baker had two shops, and George his brother was a corn merchant. They used to have the bakery at the side, up the passage, and they had a caff as well. Down where the Central is now, that used to be his shop. I can remember the man that had it before him too, that was Roach. My husband was apprenticed as a baker with him in the 1930s, but he never took to the trade. When he'd done his training, Roach offered him a job, but only at the same money as when he was an apprentice. Well, he only stopped for a bit, and then he went in the army.

Margery Hunt

We were next door to the Queen's Head in South Street, and next to that was Tucks the bakers. I used to go down the passage to the bakehouse and get a loaf while it was nice and warm. On a

Sunday, if dad wanted a bottle of cider he'd lean over the garden wall and shout for Mrs Basset in the Queen's Head. He'd hang a piece of string over, she'd tie the bottle of cider on, and he'd pull it up so that we'd have cider with our Sunday dinner. Then he'd pay her when he went in next.

Ray Fisher

There were lots of shops in Etnam Street. Coopers the cake shop, it's a gun shop now, and then just below that was a sweet shop cum grocery shop. At the very bottom was a little shop called Lewis's. You just got what you needed, tea, sugar, that kind of thing, because it was so close. There was a little old lady and I used to do her shopping all the time, one thing at a time. She dressed just like a Quaker. She had a funny hat on and a wrap-round black apron, and she didn't walk, she shuffled. She never wore anything different, the same thing every day, day in, day out.

Meryl Boff

Coopers bread shop made the most beautiful cakes. I always remember this chocolate cake they had, with all little bits of chocolate on. I've never tasted anything like it since. It was unique.

Lee McColgan

Pugh's shoe shop originally started in Etnam Street, across the road from the museum, and then they bought the shop in the High Street. We think it was 130 years old when Dad and his sister sold up, and it was used by his grandfather, Thomas Pugh,

Pugh's shoe shop – Thomas Pugh is on the left

who is in the picture, the old man. We're not sure who the other man is; it could be an uncle. We haven't a clue who the little girl is, probably somebody walking up the street who stopped and got herself in the picture. My earliest days are of the front of the shop as it is in that photograph. I can remember them putting the brand new shop front in. We had to walk across planks to get into the shop when they took the old frontage out.

I never went up into the workshop because the steps were so rickety. If a farmer came in and asked to put some studs in his boots, Dad went up there and knocked them in against the laths.

A lot of people used to come in for a chat with Dad. They'd say, 'I've had these shoes ten years, and they still haven't worn out.' Dad said, 'That's why I'm so poor, they last so long!'

The shop was huge; you walked through the door, then there was a front and a back. You walked up the passage way along Wellington Alley – they called it that because that's where they hung all their Wellingtons!

We bought a lot of our footwear from Blunts in Kidderminster, a big family wholesale fashion company. You had to order your shoes twelve months in advance, so it was a risky business, because you had to hope you had the right fashions and colours. Dad always kept his sale until the end of January; he said there's no point in having a sale if you're not going to knock the prices down. They wanted the room for the new stock to come in.

We had a living room at the back with two leather chairs and a big table, so you could see somebody coming into the shop and if you were eating your meal, it got left! I can remember them closing at lunchtimes when I was quite young and used to come to the shop for my lunch. Off the kitchen was a set of stairs up to the two workshops.

I would have loved to have carried the shop on, but they didn't ever spend any money on the building and it just went down; it would have cost too much to have put it right.

Denise Pugh

"You wore 'em a bit 'ard, han't ya?"

Seager's boot shop on the corner used to mend boots and sell them. We used to take our boots for him to mend, and he'd say, 'You wore 'em a bit 'ard, han't ya?' But he'd mend them. They'd keep repairing them until they couldn't repair them any more. There was another boot mender, Thomas, down Etnam Street; he lived in one of the little cottages by the Chequers. You'd go up the back. He only mended boots, he didn't sell them. Then in New Street there was a row of cottages, and that's where Wainwright the boot mender was. The boot shop was on the corner of High Street and Drapers Lane. It didn't have any windows, it was open, and all it sold was boots.

Margery Hunt

What I liked about Leominster was the way people would help you with things. For instance, there was a bicycle place called Coulston Davies in Etnam Street. If something happened to your bike you'd stop and ask him to have a look at it. He'd do it, but he never seemed to charge you. It was the same with Mr Evans, who had a leather shop at the top of Broad Street. Often we'd go in there and ask him to lace our football up. We never thought about paying for it. Things seemed to be a bit different in those days.

Ray Fisher

Looking for work

In the 1920s some friends of Mother's had a lovely farm. Something happened to the help they had, so I went, not intending to stay, and I stayed on there for eleven years! I can't remember the wages – about 5 shillings to start with, I think, and then it went on up to 10 shillings a week, and then a bit more and a bit more.

Elizabeth Lewis

My brother, two years older than me, he went to a hiring fair at Pembridge. You accepted a farmer's shilling and you were hired for twelve months on his farm. I didn't have a hiring fair experience, and I never had that last day at school. My father made a bit of hay and I was working at home and eventually realised I'd reached the age of fourteen. I went to my first job, strapping a case with my few things in it onto my new cycle, to Mr Mason's Lower House Farm, Wigmore.

I was engaged to look after two horses used for a milk round in the village and taking the farmer to market, as well as feeding pigs and chickens, cleaning sties, cutting wood, trimming hedges, muck spreading et cetera, not forgetting scrubbing the milk float after every delivery. I was allowed home on a Sunday once a fortnight for a change of laundry, and I had all my food and shared a bed in a back bedroom with another workman, all for 3/6 per week, not forgetting the fat bacon for breakfast.

I started at half past five or six in the morning, bringing the cows in from the pasture. And I'd help to do the milking, all by hand, no electricity; hurricane lamps in the winter. When I left in July 1936 my pay had risen to twelve shillings – poor pay, but I did at least have a job.

Herbert Millichamp

When I left school I went to see the headmaster and he asked what I wanted to do. I said I wanted to get into a garage. Things

---

Fred Parsons' Indenture for apprenticeship.

….shall not play at cards, dice, tables, or any unlawful game, shall not haunt taverns or ale houses, nor absent himself from his masters service night or day unlawfully, but in all things as a faithfull apprentice
….will instruct the apprentice in his art trade or calling of Gentlemans Hairdresser, and also pay him 2/- per week plus dinner and tea in the first year.

were bad in the 1930s and he said, 'There are no jobs like that, but there's a barber in town and he's asked me if I've got a good boy to be an apprentice in the barber's shop.' I said, 'I don't want that sort of work, sir'. Well, he told me what I was going to do, and I ended up there. There was nothing else, really. I didn't fancy being in a grocer's shop or anything like that, so I signed the apprenticeship form. I used to cycle in from Eye every day.

It was horrible at first. I had to stand watching, watching, watching. They'd give me a pair of scissors, and I had to keep a certain way of holding them. I had to keep doing this and turning the comb over – not against anybody's head. I learned to sharpen the razors. I got so that I liked it in the end.

Fred Parsons

"Work was easy to get – getting money was the hard part!"

On May hiring day, you'd stand under the clock at Knighton and they'd come and ask you, 'Do you want to hire, boy?' My first wage was £11 a year and I don't think I ever got that. I never had a pay packet; I had to give Father a few bob, and then there was a few left for me.

I went up a bit then and got a job on a farm driving horses. The farmer gave me a cheque as a sub, and it bounced, a £1 cheque bounced! Work was easy to get – getting money was the hard part! They'd threaten you in those days, threaten you, aye ...

Arthur Edwards

I was in service first, up Bargates. My sister used to work for this woman, she'd finished, and they took me on. You were on from half past six in the morning until half past nine at night. Ten shillings a month it was. I didn't like it. The woman didn't treat me like she'd treated my sister. You used to have these big red tiles in the hall. You had to Cardinal them. Well, her hall was as big as this front room. I was doing this floor, and I was doing it lovely, you know, and I thought I was nearly finished, only a couple more tiles to do. She came in – I think she'd been riding – and she said, 'Don't say you've finished; look at this, look at the mud on here.' And she put her foot on it. I could have cried! I had to do it all over again, and she stepped on every one of them, that's how she was. At half past nine at night you were still ironing the clothes. It was terrible; I only stuck it a month. I got myself a job looking after children, and I left.

Dorothy Oughton

I went into service when I was fourteen. My mother had my case ready, and my uniform. You wore blue and white in the morning, with a white cap, and in the afternoon you wore black and a little lace apron, and a white lace cap. It didn't go over your head, it went round and tied at the back. My first job was at The Cedars in Pinsley Road, Taylor's. I didn't like it at all. I had 4/6d a week, and out of that I had to give my mother a certain amount. I think I had about a shilling pocket money. We used to start at half past six. Light the fires, clean the grate, take their morning tea up. Then you'd have breakfast – they had breakfast in the dining room, but you had yours in the kitchen. I always had good food wherever I went.

Margery Hunt

I left school at fourteen, and got a job cleaning for a little while in Broad Street. They let me take Evelyn, my younger sister, with me, and the bigger ones were working in shops, so they were all right. It was quite interesting, they were really nice people. I can only remember working for Edwards and for Colonel Downes-Powell. I used to enjoy my work, and they were very good to me. They always said, 'Eileen, would you mind doing this?' or 'Would you mind doing that?' Well I mean, it makes such a difference. You don't say 'No, do it yourself!'

Eileen Bacon

I left school in about October 1937. It wasn't easy to get jobs at that time. Things were beginning to improve after the Depression, but if you could get a job, you thought you'd done pretty well. One of my pals went into a bank, and another of my friends got a job in the surveyors' office in the Town Hall. It was a question of trying to find any job rather than the kind of thing that you wanted to pursue.

It so happened that a vacancy came up in the Post Office in Leominster, and my father said it would be a good idea if I applied for it. So I did, and I had an interview, and I got the post. I wasn't keen to go into the Post Office at all. The main thing was to get a job really.

When I joined, the Post Office was part of the Civil Service, and I think I earned 17/6d for a six day week – no half days, no days off. It was far better than many jobs, I thought. In those days it was rather interesting, because you did everything. You went on the counter, in the sorting office, and you also did telegraph work. At that time there was a manual telephone exchange in the Post Office here at Leominster, and they trained us to operate it. I had to be at work sometimes at half past four in the morning, in charge of the sorting office and also the telephone exchange upstairs. You were working in the sorting office and the bell would ring and you would have to drop what you were doing and run upstairs and go and operate.

Doug Lewis

I went nannying for a schoolmaster, Mr Lee Thomas. One of the girls taught me to cook and make cakes with special icing that the children could eat, that wasn't too sweet on their teeth. When the children were older I left and went to Woolworth's. I worked there for years. Then I worked at International. There was a butcher on the end called Dewhurst, and he poached me from there. I went there for a two day trial, and stayed there, and ended up doing everything. Then that packed in so I went up to Mr Taylor, who used to have a little garage up West Street.

Dorothy Oughton

There were jobs galore – a lot to do with farming, or on the auctions. Leominster was renowned for its cattle auctions in particular. The first Monday in November and the first Monday in October we had a mighty sale in the town. It was the biggest in the country. There would be 1,100 steers, bullocks we used to call them, on the Monday, then on the Tuesday we would have 900 female cattle. Oh, it was busy! Hectic! Lots of work for lots of people in those days, always a few coppers for people to earn. In my case, I went as a butcher's apprentice. You were always wanted as a butcher, always wanted in that day and age.

Malcolm Newman

I was fourteen when off I went to an apprenticeship for four years at a farm between Tregarron and Aberystwyth. The farm was run by a brother and sister in their late forties, They only had two bedrooms, and obviously the sister had one and he had the other, but he had a nephew of fifteen years, older than me, and there were two beds there and I had to sleep with the nephew till I was 18. I got a shilling a week for the first year, then it went up – two shillings, three shillings, four shillings. I earned £25 through hard labour. I never did less than 80 hours a week. And when it was the harvest, of course it was all horses, none of these combines or balers, it had to be done with forks. I could work through the night, and he never gave me anything extra whatsoever. I left at eighteen and went up to my sister, who had a very prominent position – parlour maid to the managing director of Express Dairies. They offered me a job in London, and of course I jumped at that and off I went. I'd only been there fifteen months when war broke out, and I was conscripted in May 1940.

Alec Haines

Earning a living on the land

We had a smallholding of about nine acres. At one time my mother had four cows, and she used to do the milking, make butter, and feather the chickens and cockerels and ducks.

We used to kill one or two pigs a year. The butcher would come across when they were ready to kill, and it would take him about an hour to kill it. He'd hang it up in the back kitchen and come the next day and cut it up into hams and flitches. Very good meat as well. We used to keep most of it, but sometimes we'd give our neighbours some, and when they killed we'd get it back then.

Arthur Evans

We'd always have a bacon pig fed and killed in the winter. The pig was fed on scraps from our meals, kept in a barrel outside; it was smelly at times. There would be three slaughter men – Mr Bengree, my uncle, Mr Jack James and at Ashton Mr Percy Green. Three or four men would haul the screaming pig from the sty and hold it on the bench – no pre-stunning in those days. Just a knife and hold him until the last drop of blood had gone. Then the pig was laid out and covered with straw, and then they'd set a fire to burn the bristles off. A big pig – a smaller pig they'd use hot water to scald them off.

Herbert Millichamp

When you had a pig killed, you had to salt it to keep it. It wouldn't keep if you didn't keep it well salted.

We kept a couple of cows for the house, and made butter once a week. You'd keep the cream, more would come every day, and you'd stir it with a wooden spoon. The separators came much later. We had the old fashioned 'leads', they'd be very old. They stood on four legs, and inside it was lead, two feet wide. The milk went in every day and you separated the milk from the cream. You caught the cream in a basin and you had that for the house. It was very nice too! Most of it was for the house, but we did sell a little, what we didn't want.

How long did it take to churn butter? Well, it depended on the weather, for one thing. It would take half an hour or three quarters of an hour, I suppose, turning the handle and pressing a little thing to let the air out every now and again.

Elizabeth Lewis

I had only just turned fourteen, and putting gear on four big cart horses was a pretty big job for me. To put the big collar on I had to get up in the boosey [manger], and then after I'd put on the cart saddle, the bridle and harness and that, I'd take the horse round to where the cart was. One day I backed this horse into the cart, lifted the shares up and lit underneath his head to throw the back chain over the cart, and while I was doing that, he bit me on the arm! My brother Charlie was a waggoner and he was better than me with the horses. He could gear it up in the stables and he'd tell the horse what to do, you know. He could back him into the cart and he wouldn't put his hand on the horse. He'd just tell him. He was very good with the horses, very good.

Hay was loose, and in the fields it was cocked in cocks, ready to load. You could load the wagons three times, perhaps, in a day. I think I could put an acre on one dray. Heavy work, you never had much time, and sweaty – your trousers would stick to you. I can remember in the fields you'd hear the church clock striking – it was eleven o'clock some nights.

Arthur Evans

As kids we used to love to hang between the two wheels of the big horse-drawn wagons, and go trundling along the field underneath the wagon. Oh God! If the farmer caught us mind, we would get in a row, yes we would.

I did sheep shearing as well, but I wasn't very good at that because I was only a little chap and the big Shropshire sheep would almost lift me off the ground! When I was a kid I used to wind the wheels round for them to shear a sheep. You'd only run one cutter off that and you were about knackered when you'd finished one sheep. We did one sheep, and then we were so tired we'd have a good rest and somebody else would do it. The farmer or the shepherd would take a turn as well. We'd get through about twenty-five sheep a day. It was a long job shearing, it really was.

Then there was the old steam-powered traction engine for threshing. We loved to be around when they was threshing because we would wait for the rats to come out. There was always a crowd at the end of a bay. When you was binding a field of corn everybody from several farms would come watching, to chase them over the sheaves that the binder had left out. That was great fun.

George Oakley

There was a group of chaps who used to get their terriers and kill rats. They would put a tremendous round of netting all around a corn stack, ring the corn stubble, and start to fire it. That would drive the rats inwards and then the terriers would go in and there would be a prize for the best one. Cor! Crumbs! They destroyed them! There used to be wagers on the number of rats a terrier would kill in a certain time.

When I came out of the army in 1945, anyone would let you have a rabbit for fourpence.

Alec Haines

We got to be thankful for the rabbits. We used to catch two or three every Sunday. We'd ferret them on a Sunday, us boys'd see to that. We had two or three ferrets. You'd lay the nets on the holes, you'd hear such a rumble and if there were rabbits you would get them then. We caught most of the rabbits on our nine acres, and pinched them off our neighbours. We even tried to get them from the common on moonlight nights, but we didn't do much good.

Arthur Evans

My dad used to go poaching and that. He didn't have a gun – he wouldn't have been allowed. If you went poaching for a rabbit you'd have a big stick to hit the poor rabbit, stun it, and then finish it off and take it home.

Eileen Bacon

My mother stopped at home and looked after her dad. He'd got a little smallholding and he used to keep chickens, pigs ducks and sheep. We had some pigs, and we were having them killed just before Christmas. Dad would take us kids for a walk. He couldn't bear it, how they squealed. My mother was a proper farmer mind, she would stand there and help, and she used to do all the cutting up and jointing herself. We moved from 41 Bridge Street down to the Hundred, right at the bottom of Bridge Street; it was called The Marsh. Fosters used to have a mill down there and they had a shop on the corner of West Street going into Rainbow Street. That used to be a corn shop, and I would go and fetch a little bag of corn for my mum's chickens. She fattened them up for Christmas, and she always sent one to her sister in Manchester. We kept them for eggs, and when they was getting old, she'd kill them off.

Margery Hunt

One hobby that I had was sheepdog puppies. I used to buy pups, and I'd half break them with an older dog, and then sell them. I'd probably pay ten shillings for a pup, and sell him for a pound three months later.

We kept a few pigeons at home, we had some fantails once. Pretty birds. I was never a pigeon man myself, but there were at least six lofts around this little area alone until recent years, it was a thing that the youngsters used to do. The pigeon fanciers had a club at the Dukes Arms in Etnam Street. We always kept chickens, me and my mother between us – a partnership – we always had a chicken pen. We'd fatten cockerels up for Christmas. Everybody had chickens and you'd do a deal, go round in the evening to somebody and swap them a couple of cockerels for a couple of pullets.

Malcolm Newman

"Everybody had chickens ..."

When we lived in South Street on the Iron Cross, we had chickens in the back garden. Everybody had chickens if they had room for them.

Ray Fisher

We used to go wooding; we'd cross the fields and if the farmers had cut a tree down they'd give us all the boughs and we'd take our little chopper, chop them up, bundle up the kindling, and take it round the houses and sell it. Two bundles for three ha'pence. A lot of children used to do that to get a bit of pocket money.

Margery Hunt

Potato picking at Broadwood Hall, Leominster in 1951. Leaning on the lorry are Tommy Rogers, Gordon Hinton and Jim Stinton

People used to take washing in for the lords and ladies of the town. Mother did the washing with a dubby thing in the tub, and my job – as the eldest boy – was to take it on my arms, fold it across, mustn't stop to talk to anybody, must take it back like that, a pile of washing, to G.P. Lloyds the solicitor, or Miss Cuslett, who lived in South Street, a very nice lady. Where else? The vet's, Mr and Mrs Peatt. People like that. For coppers, you know, she would do their washing for coppers.

Malcolm Newman

Cider was the main drink on the farm. The horses would pull a big stone round and round until the apples were crunched enough to put them into the hairs to be crushed. My boss on the farm used to get rum barrels to put the cider in, and that's how it came to be so good. He'd let you have a bottle or so night and morning, or in the afternoon – it depended what you were doing. You could work with it, it gave you strength.

Arthur Evans

Most of the cider drunk in the town was made at the presses of Yeoman's Cider Factory at the bottom of Ryelands Road, where my brother Reg worked before he left the town to join the Metropolitan Police. However, a lot of cider for personal consumption by the farmers was made at co-operatives on their farms. My uncle, whose farm was about two miles north of the town, produced all sorts of fruit including apples, pears and plums, the best of which he picked by hand and sold at market. My three younger sisters and I frequently walked to the farm and helped with the picking. The casual labourers who picked the hops, potatoes, sugar beet and fruit in the fields had gang-leaders. They were mostly female, and they had considerable influence in the poorer communities, as they dictated who got work in the fields and earned money to put food on their table. The casual labourers who depended on their patronage crossed them socially or at work at their peril!

Roy Gough

There wasn't too much fruit for eating around here; it was all cider apples, and the work would be picking them up. And then people would help in the fields pulling up swedes and so forth, and on to potatoes.

There weren't many sprout fields around Leominster, but within seven miles, Canon Pyon way, there were fields and fields of them. The women would be out straight after dawn, and I used to feel sorry for them, because in the middle of winter they'd be out there and their hands must have been so cold. Yet they did it.

Alec Haines

I used to work in the fields a lot. Tater picking, currant picking, strawberry picking, I use to love that. With my currant-picking money I used to have a day out and go to Blackpool to see the lights.

Margery Hunt

Through the war, and just after, in between jobs the women went out in the fields to work. Us children, we had to go as well, even if it meant missing school. Whatever there was – picking peas, potatoes, raspberries, hops, or cider apples – because that was the only way of getting any proper money. It was hard work too, especially potato picking. The tractor went in front of you and you had to keep picking them into buckets, all the way along. It was back-breaking, absolutely back-breaking. I did blackcurrant picking when my children were little, and so did a lot of women with children. We all used to go in lorries out to The Broad, down towards Ludlow. That was quite the thing in Leominster – all through the year there was something going on.

Pauline Davies

They would use two horses to get the potatoes up, and women would come and pick them. I used to go down the row with a pony and float and pick up four bags; they were about a hundredweight. I'd take them to the other end of the field and there was a man there weighing the potatoes with the scales, and a woman stitching and tying the bags. Then a lorry would come and take them. But the women picking – it was pretty hard work for them.

Arthur Evans

Women would be regular picking potatoes. They'd come out from Leominster on their bikes – they'd have about eleven women at

Treasures doing it. You'd peg so much out for them in the morning – so they didn't cheat!

Arthur Edwards

I used to go tater picking to Sperry's at the Broad. During the war, he used to send his potatoes up country for the troops. Once Mr Sperry came to my house and asked me to get him about a dozen pickers; he had to get a load of potatoes to be picked up at nine o'clock. That was six o'clock, and I would think half Bridge Street went. When we were coming home he said he had a stack of taters sorted for the pigs, and told me to help myself. I had an old pram, so I filled this pram, and I'd got about half way home when the wheels collapsed!

Margery Hunt

When we went in the fields picking potatoes, we'd start in February and we went right up till Christmas practically. One time the farmer came over the field with lighted branches, thawing the ground out for us to pull the beet. We did it though – perhaps that's why we're suffering today!

Dorothy Oughton

Hop picking

The misty mornings and hot days of September always meant hop picking for me. Early every morning I was packed off with a bottle of tea and some cheese or spam sandwiches to meet up with my Auntie Jo and accompany her to the hop yards, travelling in a rickety old bus to the farms at Ivington.

Roy Gough

It was about four o'clock, that very first morning in September. We'd meet near a big beech tree behind the Clifton, to go hop picking. Dishley Street, Etnam Street, South Street, the estates at the back, they all used to gather together and go to Yeomans of Canon Pyon. To us as children it seemed like going to the end of the world. It wasn't like going up the road, it was seven or eight miles away! The farmer's lorry would be waiting for us, a cattle wagon with benches, and we were thrown about quite a bit.

The women that went with us, like Maggie Reynolds, Minnie Castle, and Rose Bowen, they all lived in the houses on the left hand side of Dishley Street, on the corner where Somerfield is now. All their sandwiches were packed beautifully in muslin; I don't know how they got it so white. Back in the 40s these ladies used to wear long black dresses, you know – it seems unbelievable, but they certainly did. They wore long dresses and aprons and

they were all spotlessly clean except for the fact that they took snuff. As a child I used to be absolutely appalled by that.

Pauline Davies

In one hop yard at Brierley, he had a First World War Morris 1 ton lorry, covered with canvas at the back. Now at Brierley there's a very steep bank, and several times it wouldn't go up in bottom gear, and I would have to reverse, and ask for ten or fifteen people to get off.

When I was mechanic at Bridge Street I would go and bring them in. It didn't have the modern starter, it had a magneto, and I had to start it with a handle in the front. It was a heck of a job to turn the handle – you had to get your hand right otherwise it kicked and you could break your wrist. I had to drive that darned thing for about four years.

Alec Haines

There were quite a few yards in Leominster and just out in the country, like Pasks of Endale, and Speakmans, Davies' of Brierley, Helms of Wharton. My aunts lived at the other side of the town down Bridge Street over the Canniter Bridge, so they went to Pasks of Endale. That's how it seemed to be, you seemed to go to the nearest. Quite a few went from the Crescent area and that end of the town to Helms, along the Hereford road.

Pauline Davies

We did quite a bit of hop picking for Davies' at Brierley and Helms on the main road to Hereford. There were hop fields all round here. We used to take a lorry, the dilly – we'd get in the back and it would take us out there and bring us back at night. I think they did two trips in the lorry, so you could go out early or late. I suppose you could stop there as long as you liked if you wanted to walk back. I used to go with my granny, she loved hop picking.

Ray Fisher

Speakmans at Ivington used to fetch their hop pickers at seven o'clock and half past seven in the morning on a dray and horse from the top of the Ryelands. All the people down Bridge Street and Lower Bridge Street, the Marsh as we called it, used to go. Some would walk up to Ivington from there – they wouldn't go on the dray, 'cos the horse ran away once, but it was only one little girl hurt, and she wasn't too bad.

Margery Hunt

On arrival at the farm we would stream off the bus and hurry into the hopyard, eager to 'get scrattin' or picking the hops and make as much money as possible. That early in the morning the mist would still be lying across the fields and the hop bines would be covered with damp spiders' webs, restricting visibility and giving the whole place a ghostly feeling. We would quickly find our crib in the line of cribs and compete in shouting for the farm labourers

to come and cut down some of the hop bines which towered above us, then away we would go, scrattin the hops off the bines.

Roy Gough

"No health and safety in those days ..."

First thing in the morning the children's job – right from very tiny children – was to get the bonfire going. Then we'd go into the fields. The farmers weren't worried, no health and safety in those days, they just left us to our own devices. We'd dig up the potatoes, never wash them or anything, and put them straight on the bonfire. They came out almost black with charcoal. In those days it was considered quite good for you. I don't know if it is, but they tasted out of this world. And we had long sticks and we would wind bacon round them, although bacon was not very easy to obtain. The smell through the hop yards is something I still remember.

The young children, four or five, used to pick in upside-down old umbrellas by the side. You had to do something. There was no such thing as going off to play, it was very rare. When we were allowed to, we used to pick sloes, and they tasted horrible, and climb the apple trees in the orchard close by.

Pauline Davies

Even though we were children we had to do our turn as well. We'd have cardboard boxes in front of us to pick into, and Dad would make us a little stool – just a piece of plank across – and we'd sit and pick the hops, and then throw them into the crib. We had to do our fair share, we weren't allowed to play around.

In the morning the weather would often be dull and then in the afternoon it would be so hot. We used to try to keep a couple of the wires up so we'd have a bit of shade. It was hurtful when you had to wait until somebody came to move your crib into another place, so you could shelter from the sun. We had the hottest summers. We never wore a coat or shoes. We had sandals all through the summer, from Easter right through to the end of September. Never knew what a coat was like, or a cardigan.

Dorothy Oughton

The mothers used to pick the 'reams' or 'house,' which were the aisles of hops, and they chose the crib they wanted. The crib was made of sacking with four posts holding it up, and if there were two of you picking, say mother and daughter, or mother and sister, there was a partition in the middle and you picked ends. When I was about nine I had half a crib with my mother, I took ends with my mother, and the first time I was so proud of myself. I earned £1 10s, which was a lot of money. I bought a galvanised bath to go in front of the fire with it.

I should think the hop bines were about six foot high, perhaps a bit more. They would cut the bine at the bottom with a knife, and then you would hang on to it until it came down. I couldn't have done it when I was a child because you had to be fairly strong to pull them down. If you had any problems, there was generally a busheller around or somebody who would come and give a hand to the women. You just held the spray in your left hand and picked the sprays of hops off the bines; you scratched them off, as they used to say.

The bushellers would move you when you wanted to be moved, and it was the children's job to pick up the hops on the floor and get the leaves out of the crib. They wouldn't have a single hop on the floor, and they wouldn't have a leaf in the crib. You had to get those leaves out or they wouldn't accept it.

Pauline Davies

My auntie would stand at the crib all day, stripping the hops off the bines, only stopping when waiting for more bines or to be moved, or for refreshments. I can see her now, dressed in an apron with a turban on her head, a Woodbine in her mouth and her hands darting back and forth as she picked the hops. It was not only back-breaking work and the money hard earned, but the hops had a strong sour smell and stained the hands dark brown.

Roy Gough

When my mother was hop picking and she wanted fresh bread, there was a baker down here called Saunders and I used to go there to get the bread. Then I'd walk all the way out to Ivington, and I was only seven. You couldn't do it now, the children can't do it.

Dorothy Oughton

The highlight of the day was a van that used to come down from Saunders, the bakers. They used to bring fresh cakes and bread, and that was lovely, really lovely. For tea my mother and her friends had a very old black kettle and that would go on the fire, because that was the only way we could make a cup of tea.

Pauline Davies

They'd make a fire to boil the kettle, and throw the potatoes in to bake. There was a woman who had this biscuit tin, and she put it on its side somehow. She had it fixed so that she could put the kettle on the top and boil it, and do her cooking. She would cook all different kinds of things. If your crib happened to be near hers, the smell when she used to cook …

Phyllis Manson

"Have you ever seen a hedgehog when it's been roasted?"

Yeomans had the Eastenders from London. It was their holiday, and they would come and mix with all the locals. They probably went down to the local pub at night and had a wonderful time singing. And of course there were a lot of painted caravans, with

the gypsies. There was a lot of gypsies and they stayed throughout the year, for the potato picking, hop picking, or whatever the farmer was growing at the time.

Pauline Davies

Have you ever seen a hedgehog when it's been roasted? There was a gypsy man named Malpiard and he was picking by us when he asked to use our fire, to roast this hedgehog. They killed them, left them in their skin and put them in the fire. When the hedgehog was done, they'd get it in the ashes and just cut the top and strip it right off, till it was nothing but a lump, like a chicken's breast. Malpiard said it was all he'd got to eat that day. If he didn't get fieldwork he had no money, and his children had to live on roast hedgehog. I did try some, and it was lovely.

Margery Hunt

Luckily for me I didn't stand at the crib all day but got all the odd jobs – and there were many. I would fetch the labourers when more bines needed cutting down or the crib needed moving, carry the bags and other personal stuff to the new location, run errands, find firewood, light the fire and make the tea for lunch. Finding firewood was the best fun, because while doing this I could hunt for potatoes, turnips or swedes for the evening pot, or play in the barns and search for eggs.

The tea that I made there was like no other that I've tasted since. Once the kettle had boiled, my auntie would put a twist of tea leaves in it and leave it to stew for a while. Then I would add thick condensed milk, leave it again for a few minutes and then pour it into tin mugs. With its strong smoky taste it was much better than the cold tea from the bottle – and it wasn't difficult to spit the tea leaves out.

Roy Gough

When I was a kid we always went out to Endale, to Treasures on the Ludlow road. We used to walk out there. He was a hard man, but fair. He wouldn't give you *that*, but he was fair. He didn't like you running about the hopyard, he liked you in, but we always used to have a play, you know, a break. He'd say, 'Now, you're *not* to go in the orchard.' 'No Mr Treasure, no sir.' 'If I catch you in the orchard,' he said, 'I'll turn you off the ground.' And he would have done it.

Margery Hunt

My mother was a very hard, harsh woman. You did *exactly* what she said, like a lot of mothers in those days. In the hopyards she'd say, 'You can go and play for half an hour.' If you weren't back at the half hour, they had what we called a bine by the side of the crib. Couple of cuts! Did no harm. But it was a harsh life, very harsh – believe it.

Malcolm Newman

My granny lived out at Dilwyn and she wanted us out there to pick for her, so I had to go. She'd insist that I stayed at that crib all day long, picking. I'd say to her, 'I need to go to the toilet' and of course I'd go off and I wouldn't come back till the end of the day. You'd have brown fingers, and there was the smell of hops, I loved it. Oh, I've got happy memories of hop picking.

Lee McColgan

I used to go out with my bicycle to a hopyard for my mother-in-law at four o'clock in the morning. I'd get a good crib and a nice place. I had four jars with four candles in, till it became light. I'd be picking and then my wife and some of her friends would come out and pick there too. On Sunday I would go out in the afternoon and pick a lot, but you see, I shouldn't have done that, I would have to cover them over with a sack, to hide them until Monday.

In one hopyard there would be hundreds of children, picking and playing. When the Yeomans bus came winding its way past the hopyard they would run to the heads, because the bus had its radio on. It would only go about four miles up a hill and turn around again, and it was a fantastic sight to see all these children cheering. They wouldn't have had a radio at home, and to think that a radio was on a bus!

Alec Haines

"It was a harsh life, very harsh ..."

We didn't go to school for at least two weeks into the autumn term because of hop picking. It was lovely. In those days there was what they called the 'Bomber' coming round looking for children who should have been at school. Some of the mothers used to be terrified that they were going to come and catch them. I don't think there was a fine or anything, but I know some children were dragged back.

Pauline Davies

That was one way of getting extra holidays off school, going out into the fields. I could never understand why they didn't work it so that children were off school during that period. The majority of the kiddies used to stay home from school anyway.

Phyllis Manson

We all had to do our share and work hard. Mother had the bit of money that was earned, and fitted us three boys out for school. One year she turned round and said 'Good gracious! I've got enough out of the money to buy myself a pinafore.'

Malcolm Newman

The hops were in a line, you had so far, and there was a marker in the ground. All those were yours; you couldn't pick anybody else's. Once you'd picked those, they'd come along and move your crib to another place. Sometimes you couldn't pull the bines down or the string wouldn't break. A chap would come along with a hook that was sharp on the inside, and he'd hook it over and cut the top. Then you just pulled them down and picked them into your crib. The chap came round and bushelled them in a big basket. He had a book and he'd write down how many bushels you'd got. They were eleven pence or a shilling a bushel, something like that – it wasn't much. We were always saying 'You ought to be giving us an extra tuppence a bushel for them', but they never did.

At the end there was a nice lump sum which always came in handy. Gran would reward us with something, a football or something like that. It wasn't much really, but I suppose we didn't do an awful lot of work. Most of the time we were running off round the fields, just enjoying ourselves, but we always used to pick quite a few hops. My gran used to expect us to do a bit of work.

Ray Fisher

You might move your crib and be under a rotten lot of hops. The pay was so much a bushel, and it was measured by volume. A bushel had quite a wide top, slightly elongated down, and two

Hop picking at Upper Wall End, Monkland at the end of the season in 1937, when fair weather had produced a good quality crop. The crib is full of hops and the busheller is emptying his basket into a pocket

handles. The busheller would press it down with his elbow if he could get away with it, to get more in. The measure was for hops without too many leaves, so if people had too many leaves in the sample, he wouldn't take it, and they had to get more leaves out. Some would then tell him that he must have gone to his father's and mother's wedding – and all those sort of things. The busheller was the most unpopular man on the hopyards. He was the worst chap ever in the world!

Alec Haines

I think the busheller came round about twice a day. You got some really good bushellers, and some that weren't so nice. On the last day of hop picking, if they weren't very popular they were pushed into the cribs and they didn't have a very good time. The last day was always a good day because that was the payday and people would go up to the kilns and get their money. They had cards and as the busheller would say ten bushels, and write it down on the card. The pickers watched him like a hawk, because some of the bushellers were very much on the farmer's side. There was one lady, Rose Hall, and if there were bushellers they weren't very happy with she used to get the pickers to go on strike for an extra sixpence. The women were very forceful in those days. Well they had to be, it was wartime and they had to earn a living. You can imagine there was hell to pay if they had a ream or a house [see page 99] that had what they call 'beady hops,' little brown hops.

Pauline Davies

The doctor used to charge five shillings and sixpence to attend. You had your doctor's bill every three months, and I usually had one just before hop picking. I used to think, 'Well, I've earned my doctor's bill now, and what I earn after that is mine.' We would rig the kids out with them, or buy some coal for the winter.

Margery Hunt

My mother had to go hop picking because they paid very good money – well, it was considered good in those days. It was very hard work. My mother had £1 10 shillings a week army pay and she only had me, so it wasn't so bad, but there was quite a few who had less. Hop picking was quite an event, and I don't think there were many women, unless they were very wealthy, who didn't go. Even if they had small jobs, they would go hop picking and make some excuse not to do their other job in that time. I think my mother would have earned about £30 for the whole five weeks. That paid for the school uniform and helped us during the winter. That's why they went, because it did help considerably. They looked forward to hop picking; it was the only way they could earn a decent wage.

Pauline Davies

In one hopyard where my wife was, when people were waiting for the busheller and their crib was full they would go over and put into these two cribs for charity. I don't know if that was practised everywhere.

Alec Haines

Eventually the long tiring day would come to an end and we would hear the farm workers shouting 'Clear 'em up'. Everyone would frantically clean their crib of leaves before the farm workers came round and collected the hops. They tallied the day's pick by measuring the hops with bushel bags, payment eventually being paid for how many bushels were picked. Once filled and tied, the bags were loaded onto a wagon pulled by two huge horses, and when the wagon was full, the load was taken to the kiln for drying.

When everyone's crib had been emptied it was time to go home – and that was a great relief. We would stream back onto the bus and slump exhausted into our seats. It wouldn't be long, however, before someone began to sing, and for me that was the best part of the day. I was a very keen singer and would frequently lead the impromptu choir, although I often didn't understand the true meaning of the songs.

A favourite melody was 'She'll be coming round the mountains when she comes', particularly the verses that included her wearing the various women's unmentionables. Another favourite was 'Roll me over in the clover', which I thoroughly enjoyed and sang with gusto as I knew it was naughty, but I didn't really understand what it meant.

Roy Gough

They had drying houses for hops. A great big fire, and the hops were laid on perforated flooring above for the heat to come up and dry them. Then they were put in huge sacks, over three yards long. Very often the farmers had to hold on to them until the market needed them.

Alec Haines

At the end of hop picking, whatever day we finished we used to get paid on a Saturday. We walked up there in our Sunday best, and the farmer would put on a lovely tea for us kids. They put forms out, and long tables, and we sat and had our tea. And then there was a barn full of apples, and you could take as many as you wanted. Then we used to walk home.

Margery Hunt

As you get older, you only remember the good times. You forget all the bad days when your arms used to hurt, all the scratches on your arms and the pollen from the hops getting into the cuts. It wouldn't be allowed today, but in all the years I went I can't remember any real accidents, not a thing.

Pauline Davies

Market days

After they had been sold, herds of cattle were driven down Etnam Street to the railway station for transport to their new homes, or on past the station to the slaughterhouse. Controlled by professional drovers who were the roughest of the rough and who I always found very frightening, the cattle charged through the town with their heads down and fear in their eyes, bellowing like banshees and emptying their bowels all over the roads and pavements. There was no consideration for pedestrians; they had to keep out of the way of the cattle and try to avoid the mess they left behind.

Roy Gough

People would drive the cattle in to market on the roads, and bring them home for you, even if it was six or seven miles. Marvellous, isn't it, to think that they could do that! Now of course they'd have to have vans or lorries to put them in.

Elizabeth Lewis

You would see them coming along the Worcester road or down Bargates, droves of cattle – thirty or forty in a bunch. After they'd been sold the majority went by rail. They were taken all over the country for fattening, Scotland, you name it – anywhere in the country from Leominster.

That was one of my favourite jobs. A gentleman named Charles Fletcher, Bunter his nickname was, he was the supremo. He dealt with the big dealers that came and bought the cattle. It was a job for a dozen boys; I'd be one, taking them down to the station. You'd have perhaps six or eight bunches of cattle between the station and the market. Your main job was keeping the bunches from mixing. All the way up and down Etnam Street, on until midnight, people in the pubs looking out, the cows mooing, and then loading them up at the station. Hectic times, particularly the October and November sales. As far as I knew then, they were the biggest cattle sales in the country, because this was a massive cattle area, Hereford cattle.

Bunter would get all the boys outside the station when the last load went on – he wouldn't pay anybody until then – and then he'd hand us our bit of the money. The little boys had a shilling, and the bigger boys, which I was by then, two shillings. That was the one night Mother didn't mind me being out very late. I was forgiven because I was working for Bunter! I'd go home proudly – I'd got two shillings to spend! I can remember I was almost afraid to spend it. I might get a pennyworth of toffee – you could get five toffees for a penny then – or some aniseed balls for a ha'penny.

Malcolm Newman

LEOMINSTER MARKET.

G.W. & L.M. & S. Railways.

Great Annual SHOW & SALE of

Store Cattle & Sheep

AND

Pedigree Hereford Bulls

CASH PRIZES £27 CASH PRIZES.

Edwards, Russell & Baldwin

Will SELL BY AUCTION, in their

Stock Yards, Leominster, on

MONDAY, MAY 3rd, 1926.

UPWARDS OF

1,125

Excellent 1 year and 2 years old **Steers,
Barren Cows and Heifers,** chiefly
Herefords, direct from the Breeders of this
Noted Stock-rearing District, in suitable Lots
for Feeding and Summer Grazing.

3 Classes, £18 Cash Prizes for Stock Exhibited & Sold.

ALSO

51 Grand Pedigree Hereford Bulls

COWS & CALVES & YEARLING HEIFERS,

When Prizes will be offered for the best Yearling Bull Exhibited
and SOLD.

First Prize, £3; Second Prize, £2; Third Prize, £1.

ALSO

600 Store Tegs & Ewes with their Lambs

Prizes for the best 20 Ewes and their Lambs Exhibited and SOLD.

First Prize, £2; Second Prize, £1.

JUDGING AT 10.30 a.m.

Sale commencing with Bulls at 11 o'clock Prompt.

Leominster, Hereford, Tenbury Wells and Hay.

LEOMINSTER PRINTING CO.

They had a special market for store cattle, we used to have up to a thousand cattle up here. When I was working in the barber's shop, we used to get a buyer from Northumberland who was in Leominster buying cattle. He used to stay overnight and come for a haircut and shave, then he'd buy these cattle and drive them off down Etnam Street to the station and load them up there. Etnam Street would be full of cow muck, it was a terrible mess.

Fred Parsons

The cattle market was where Somerfield's supermarket is now. The drovers would take the cattle right down through Etnam Street, load them on to the wagons at the station, and dash off back for another lot, perhaps having a pint of beer on the way.

Alec Haines

*This market for store cattle in Dishley Street, conducted by
Edwards, Russell and Baldwin, was reckoned to be the largest in
England in 1936*

Sheep market in 1938. The houses of Dishley Street (now demolished) are on the left

You wouldn't believe the mess! And the smell! All down the street, the drovers didn't care whether it was the road or the pavement. You had to pick your way across Etnam Street, South Street and the Bargates.

We used to go up to Mrs Heller in the Bargates for groceries, she'd got a little shop just by the infant school. This particular day I was going up and I'd got my brother by the hand. I suppose he'd have been three years old, he was walking anyway, but he wasn't very big. We got up just above Norgrove's Yard, that's just above where the BUPA Home is now. I think there were four cottages there whose doors opened onto the pavement. As we got up by these houses there was a shout to make haste and get into the gateway there, because there was a cow in the entry on the other side of the road, and it had gone wild. I got about half way along these four cottages and this cow came back down this entry, straight across the pavement at me. Anyway, somebody opened the door and took me in, and the cow hit the door rather than hitting me across the chest. I was carrying my brother by then, and we would both have been killed. It was very frightening. I wouldn't go near a cow after that. Even today I won't go near a cow.

Minnie Davies

All along Dishley Street there were old cottages, and their doors opened like a stable door, so you could open one half and lean over and have a natter to your neighbour. Now, porker pigs would be driven down Dishley Street to market, filling the road and the pavement, because it was much narrower than today. If anyone wanted a nice pig for dinner they would leave the bottom part of

the door ajar, and in would go a pig. This would happen at eleven o'clock in the morning and within six hours that pig was killed and cut up. The chaps driving them down wouldn't miss one pig, they were in a desperate hurry to put them on the trains, on their way to butchers in London or Birmingham. It was cobbled stones in those days on the pavement, and that evening they would get an old gramophone and they'd be dancing and they would have this lovely dinner. Because it was killed, cut up and hidden in no time, the police would never have caught them.

Alec Haines

Leominster was a market town, and my father's business provided for the farming fraternity. The town was extremely busy on Friday – it was market day, and all the people from the countryside used to come in. The trains used to come in from Kington and Bromyard, and you would see lots of people walking up Etnam Street. Of course my father knew a lot of them. There was a gentleman who kept the local inn at Stoke Prior, and he would call in and have a word with my father. It was arranged that if I wanted to go for a cycle ride with my friends we could call in at the pub and have some pop and crisps, and then the gentleman would call and see Father on market day, and Father would settle up with him. Very nice.

John Sharp

A farmer or smallholder, say at Kingsland, four miles out, would drive his cow in to be sold. He wouldn't have milked it the night before, to make the udder look much larger. Perhaps it was unsold, or perhaps somebody bought it and had to take it home,

The Bargates before the development of the inner ring road. The Bull's Head is at the top of West Street with stabling to the rear.
To the left is the archway leading to the sheep market

so they'd have to walk four miles with a cow with an overladen udder. So they would tie the cow to the tree in the Bargates and milk it in a pail and give milk to the people that wanted some. Oh, it was lively.

Alec Haines

On a Friday they used to have another market besides the cattle market. You could go in there and buy eggs and vegetables, all fresh brought in, and chickens and everything. They sold them by auction, but some of them would sell it to you before the auction started. You could get a cabbage and a dozen eggs and they'd last. It was so different. People used to crowd into Dishley Street on

Burgess Street – the market building behind the Town Hall on Broad Street

a Friday. You wouldn't go anywhere else, you'd go there first. The bus station used to be opposite there, and people used to come off their buses from out in the country, and wait there for the bus to go back. The buses used to stop outside the Grapes. My gran always caught her bus outside there to go to Pembridge, and they were ramshackle, shaky old buses. Wooden seats and all that. Bengry's buses, we always had Bengry's buses.

Dorothy Oughton

Leominster had these wonderful markets on a Tuesday and a Friday. On a Friday you couldn't walk up Etnam Street, it was thronged. You had a devil of a job to walk up High Street – no cars or even a bicycle could come up at all, it was jam-packed with people from the country all going about their business. Leominster was absolutely busting. Alongside the Town Hall in Burgess Street was a covered way, and on Friday the ladies from the country would bring in dressed chickens and dressed rabbits, and butter and cheese, and sell in there. It was marvellous, and of course we've lost it all.

Alec Haines

When I first remember the market it was in what was the Town Hall at the top of Broad Street. It had the clock tower on the top, and the market was underneath. They had all sorts of stalls down there. I used to come with my mother from Berrington Eye station; she came in once a week on a Friday to do the shopping. Different farmers had stalls; there was a cake stall I liked, because I always had a bun bought from there.

Fred Parsons

When I was a child we were fortunate in that we had our own milk. We'd have one or sometimes two milking cows, and we would rear the calves up to a certain age and sell them. Mother used to make butter and sell it sometimes in the market in Leominster. She borrowed a pony and trap from Miss Proudman next door to drive into town, and sometimes we would be lucky enough to go with her, but not always. I know one day I followed her, oh, a quarter of the way into Leominster. In the end she gave in and let me ride. Another pleasure to remember, if we were fortunate enough to be taken to town on market day in the pony and trap or later on the local buses, would be a visit to Pewtress Tea Rooms in Broad Street for a cup of tea and a Chelsea bun. That was a big thing.

Herbert Millichamp

"It wouldn't be Friday if you didn't come to Leominster."

We always came to Leominster on a Friday. It wouldn't be Friday if you didn't come. We'd come in a pony and trap. My husband always had such wild horses that when they were waiting to start

they'd go up on their hind legs, and I had to sit still. We used to go in at about eleven o'clock and come back at about three in the afternoon. That was our day out. You'd get your tea and sugar and cheese – not all packaged like it is now. You'd go to the shop and tell them what you wanted, and they'd cut the cheese with a wire, and cut the butter. They'd put the tea in packets – some sort of stiff paper – and they didn't stick it down or anything; they could work it in and turn it. Then they would send it down to the car or the trap. We didn't have accounts; we paid as we had it.

Elizabeth Lewis

The Butter Market was lovely. As kids we would come home from school at twelve o'clock on a Friday and we'd go through the market in the old Town Hall to see what was there. Every Friday a woman used to sit out there with a pram and sell the *Leominster News*. She sat there in all weathers and she wouldn't go until she'd sold every one. Another woman sold tea and cakes and that.

Then at Christmas it was a sight. There used to be the dead poultry market at night, and a bit before that was the livestock. They had all the hens with the little chicks in cages for sale, and rabbits. Meat was a luxury. Half the kids in Leominster would have starved if there hadn't have been rabbits about, because they couldn't afford any other meat.

Margery Hunt

You could go and have a walk round the market and everything was for sale there. People used to have chickens in their back gardens then, especially during the war. You could have eggs, you could buy chicks in a box and things like that.

The market brought trade to the town. The pubs did a roaring trade on a Friday. It was rowdy, and if a farmer had had a good day he could celebrate a bit. I can't remember any real incidents, but I'm sure there must have been times when things got a bit out of hand. The Bulls Head was a big meeting place for the country people on a Friday because it was right next to the market.

Ray Fisher

People would bring in their ponies and traps, to get their weekly groceries. There was a hotel, a big pub called the Red Lion down Broad Street, and they parked there, and at the Royal Oak as well, and they would charge sixpence to look after the horses. A chap called Morgan used to park his pony and trap down at the Red Lion, and he would get absolutely stone drunk! Somehow somebody or other would help him, and that pony and trap used to come down Etnam Street. The old pony would take him all the way home! It would be what, five and a half miles?

Alec Haines

Part Two
The Second World War

The Second World War started rather slowly in Leominster. It was remembered by many by the issuing of gas masks to the civilian population before the declaration of war, and in an echo of another conflict, the mobilisation of Territorial soldiers. Following the Blitz evacuees started to arrive from the industrial cities, first singly, and then by the trainload, as even schools were moved wholesale.

The town was declared an army garrison, and in turn the South Wales Borderers, the Hallamshire Battalion, the 2nd Battalion of the Essex Regiment, the 2nd Royal Ulster Rifles, and the 5th Suffolk Regiment were billeted in houses and requisitioned buildings.

By 1942 the town had been transformed, and many people had been directed to war work in places like the Rotherwas Munitions factory or called up for the forces. As the threat of the blitz diminished evacuees started to return home, and at about the same time American forces moved into the town. As well as using the town as a garrison base for troops, they built a large hospital at Barons Cross to treat D-Day casualties.

When secondary education became compulsory in 1944 the first Secondary Modern School was created with classes scattered in the Church Institute (now British Legion), the Scout Hall, the Masonic Hall, and other sites as well as temporary huts built in the grounds of the Church School. For a time this school also used the former American and Polish army camp in Green Lane, and later this was developed to become the main site for the Secondary School.

Residents who were children at the time remember this as a golden age of freedom and adventure. With husbands away and struggling to make ends meet on an Army allowance, their mothers probably saw it differently.

War comes to Leominster

One day in about 1934, I was looking at the newspaper. My father used to take the *Daily Telegraph* and the main headline was probably the Test match score in Australia. I thought life was quite peaceful. My mother was born in 1885, and she told me that there was no comparison between life pre-1914 and life as I knew it. She said, 'You have no idea what a peaceful life is like.' That really puts things in a bit of context.

Doug Lewis

Mrs Humphreys used to live at 127 Etnam Street. She was a war widow of the First World War, and she used to take in lodgers. This lodger that she had just prior to the war was a German, I think his name was Turlon, and he used to have a nice little sports car. He went toitering around the district, and he never seemed to do any work. The question was, when war was declared, was the lodger a spy? He left the district some months before war started. They obtained the German Army records after the end of the war and there was all sorts of useful information about Britain ... Of course it is possible, but there again you can't really tell.

John Sharp

The gloom had been descending upon us for over a year. I can remember the conversation of the grown-ups at the time about the Czechoslovakian crisis, and Munich. There was so much seriousness in the conversation that we lads, although we were only seven or eight, were very impressed.

I can remember the day, 1st September 1939, when we heard that Hitler had entered Poland. I had gone walking with friends in Newtown Lane. It was a beautiful morning, lovely. I'm not sure whether I heard the news then or later in the day, but the delightful day walking to Newtown Lane sticks very vividly in my mind.

I also remember two days later when Neville Chamberlain announced the ultimatum, otherwise there would be war. We did not have a radio at the time, but sometime in the day the news got through.

Mervyn Bufton

On 3rd September 1939, I listened with my parents to Neville Chamberlain, the Prime Minister, on the radio when he announced that from eleven a.m. that day we would be at war with Nazi Germany. That afternoon I went with my mother and her sister to the drill hall in New Street to see the Territorial

THE DECLARATION OF WAR. HOW NEWS WAS RECEIVED IN LEOMINSTER.

When Sunday morning's fateful announcement came it created a deep impression but was received with complete calm. There were some indications of excitement, noticeably a group of youngsters gathered around a loud speaker who cheered enthusiastically, when the Prime Minister's statement that a state of war existed between England and Germany.

There was certainly no evidence of a spirit of gloom. People felt that the worst had come to the worst and that the need of the moment was to meet the situation with determination and calmness.

A large number of mothers, fathers and young women went to the Drill Hall to see their sons and sweethearts in the Territorials and wish them good-bye.

Leominster News September 8th 1939

Soldiers going off to war. Dressed in the uniforms of the previous war, they were equipped with Lee Enfield rifles of that period. They had no transport other than two lorries commandeered to take them to the Regimental Depot in Shrewsbury. This was how the war started in Leominster.

Leominster was a quiet market town and then suddenly there was a great influx of people. You had the evacuees pouring in; you had people – wealthy people – who were living in say Birmingham or London, who had contacts. In my family my Aunt Clara came to stay with my father. I think at the time she was living at Walthamstow. The whole nature of the town changed.

At the time of Dunkirk they were taking them off the boats and putting them on railway trains. These poor men didn't come back in order; the idea was to get them back and find them accommodation. If I remember correctly, on one particular day at the time of Dunkirk a couple of army lorries came up from the station with some men who looked as if they'd had a hell of a rough time.

John Sharp

When they came back from Dunkirk, some lorry loads came through Leominster, and they were a pitiable sight. They were dejected; they were dirty, unkempt, slovenly – and then one heard the story. My father came home at lunchtime from the printing press. He said there were a couple of our soldiers walking across the Corn Square when an aircraft flew over, and they threw themselves on the ground. They were still reacting as if they were over there in France.

Mervyn Bufton

Some men came into the shop for a tidy up after Dunkirk. I can't remember them being that dirty, but they were so tired. They were falling asleep, just worn out.

Fred Parsons

There was a thanksgiving service for the survival of the British Army at Dunkirk. I went to that service with my parents, at the Priory. The vicar was the Reverend Moeran. He had been a chaplain in the First World War and he was there with all his medal ribbons on.

John Sharp

"Of course it was an age of hero worship."

The roads were quiet. There was the occasional delivery van, and Melia the oil merchant (he had a shop on West Street) would occasionally pass delivering oil to the villages around Leominster. The two doctors, Dr Kingdom and Dr Thompson, of course had to pay visits to different parts of town. The baker pulled a hand cart. The milkman had a pony and trap. There was hardly anything else. We boys had the streets to ourselves. We could lash our spinning tops all the way down Bargates and West Street, being careful not to smash one into a window!

Of course it was an age of hero worship. I followed the progress of the war, and it was a great time to be a boy. Every Saturday morning we fought the Second World War over the fields of Leominster. We would divide into two groups, the target being to take Cursneh Hill. One day they'd be the Jerries and we'd be the Brits, and another day it'd be the other way round. We'd have to make our way across the fields, unobserved, crawling in the ditches, getting behind the screen of bushes, using fieldcraft.

Mervyn Bufton

A gang of us used to go to play on the Easters and Eaton Hill, Cowboys and Indians, all sorts of things. In the area where the soldiers trained they'd dug some trenches. We decided that we would occupy two of the trenches, and we'd be throwing hand grenades, clumps of clay at each other. Unfortunately one of the lads got hit, I think there was a certain amount of blood, and he went running home to his mother.

John Sharp

We could play anywhere. I would go off and collect other people, and we would play all around the Newlands area. When I got a little older I used to walk for miles on my own. We lived next door to a house which had an extremely tall tree; in Leominster you can see it for miles. I used that as my landmark, so I could go anywhere and find my way home again as long as I could see the tree. I'd walk right across to Eaton Hill or head out towards Canon Pyon. I'd be out all day, and as long as I was back for tea nobody would worry about me at all.

Maureen Crumpler

The infant school was in Bargates, and during the war we'd carry our gas masks over our shoulders and take them to school. The headmistress was Mrs Maddox, quite strict as far as I can remember. Behind where we lived in Hampton Gardens it was just open land all the way to Cranes Lane in the distance. I can remember walking along with friends – we'd have been about five years old – along Perseverance Road and down the steps into Green Lane. There was some bars along there that we used to swing around on.

Ray Watkins

On the way to school we would have to cross Bargates to get to the infant school. There would be very long convoys of military vehicles heading off towards Wales, on manoeuvres or something like that. You could stand for five or ten minutes and sometimes you'd hear the school bell, and know you were going to be late, but you couldn't cross the road because they were just nose to tail heading westwards.

Maureen Crumpler

During the war, entertainment like the May Fair was stopped. But there was a Mr Hill, he had a fair and I understand he was a cousin of Billy Butlin, and he came to Leominster. He knew there was parking here, and he got permission to park all his vans and everything at the side of the yard. During the war he was engaging in timber haulage, and then when it came to the end of the war, he was allowed to set up his dodgems in the yard.

John Sharp

We had a fair at the bottom of Etnam Street all through the war years, at the White Lion. They seemed to allow the lights of the fair, and put them out at a certain time of night.

Pauline Davies

Evacuees

The school was evacuated en masse by tram into the centre of Liverpool and then by train during the morning of Friday, 1st September 1939, eventually arriving at Leominster, a totally unheard of and unknown place. It was the first of two trains from Liverpool that day, and was followed by two more the next day.

On arrival each evacuee, who had only one string and brown paper parcel of personal clothing and a cardboard box containing a gas mask, was given 'rations' for the first 48 hours, corned beef, condensed milk, etc. in a brown paper carrier bag. These were put together by the Leominster Women's Voluntary Service and were handed out on the railway platform.

Account written by an anonymous evacuee from Liverpool

The Forbury in Church Street was taken over to provide hostel accommodation for ladies and children who had come from Liverpool, the most heavily bombed city next to London. Once the bombing had eased, most of these ladies went back.

They did a survey of what people had in the way of bedroom accommodation in the town, and if you had accommodation you had to take somebody. Mr Smith, who was the local Sanitary Inspector, was the billeting officer for Leominster. After the war he told me it was the worst job he ever had in his life. It's the old, old story: if you were hoity-toity and you were allocated a couple of snotty-nosed lads, it didn't go down very well.

John Sharp

The first train of evacuees arrived in the morning and were 'billeted' within Leominster itself. I remember being taken, along with others, to a low-ceilinged, church-hall type building, where there were mounds of clothes piled onto trestle tables, from which items were extracted as needed. I will always be grateful to

A copy of this photograph of the Liverpool evacuees on the Grange shortly after their arrival was given to each boy to send home to show that he had arrived safe and sound. The teacher on the left is 'Spike' Robson, and the only pupil named is Dennis Dickinson, fourth from the left in the front standing row

This evacuee (on the right) was billeted with the Ross family at Perseverance Road. John Ross, the younger of the two sons of the family, stands on the left. The elder son, Douglas, was in the RAF and was killed during the very early weeks of the war. He is commemorated on the Leominster War Memorial at the Grange

Leominster, and in particular to the Ross family, as I was billeted with them at the very end of Perseverance Road. Their elder son, Douglas, was in the RAF and was killed during the very early weeks of the war. Miss Ross, who lived close by in a house in Green Lane, and whose garden adjoined the Rosses', also took in an evacuee. The Ross family had several shoe shops, the main one being at 17/19 High Street.

Account written by an anonymous evacuee from Liverpool

An unusual evacuation to the town was Stanley Gibbons, the stamp people, who came to Corn Street. Later in the war, the Sir George Monoux Grammar School, from Leyton, London, was relocated to Leominster after spending some time in Bromyard. My parents had two boys from the school, Len Baxter and Charlie Stringer. I think both of them came back to see my mother after the war. Later one of the boys was rehoused with another family. The evacuated school shared the Leominster Grammar School with local pupils. They had the use of the school buildings on Tuesday, Thursday and Saturday, and the local pupils had it for the other three days of the week. At the beginning of this arrangement my class (1B) were given homework for Tuesdays and had games on Thursdays. Later we had the use of the Friends' Meeting House in South Street and the Primitive Methodist Church in Green Lane. The two schools worked well together. At one time the Monoux School contributed five players to Leominster Grammar School's First XV, making it about the best rugby team in the county.

Early in 1941 some of the masters of the two schools came together to raise a Leominster Squadron, Air Training Corps,

which was designated 145 Squadron. The idea was to provide pre-training for young men who would be joining the RAF in a couple of years' time. During certain evenings of the week the cadets would study Morse Code, navigation, wireless, engines and aircraft recognition. On Sunday mornings there was a parade for foot drill at the Grammar School. The following masters were involved in the training: Mr V. Randall, Mr T. Howard, Mr Lee Thomas, Mr Minnim and Mr Phillips. A Captain Hibbert was

Leominster Squadron Air Training Corps at Leominster Station before departing to RAF Hixon Staffordshire in 1944.
Back row, left to right: John Pugh, ? , ? Berry, ? , ? Berry, 'The Prof', John Lewis, ?, ?, Kenneth Watkins.
Front row: Nelson Slaymaker, Johnny Allan, ? , ? , Mr W. Lee Thomas (Leominster Grammar School), John Sharp, ? , John Ross, David Conod, ?

appointed acting Commanding Officer with the rank of Flight Lieutenant. A large special building was built for the ATC alongside the Grammar School pavilion in the school field.

John Sharp

There were quite a few evacuees in Leominster. We had a Mrs Brown and her baby. Unless you had a very good reason, you were forced to take someone, if you had the room. They more or less came to your door and said, 'You will take these.' We only had a two-bedroom cottage, and Mum could have refused, but she wouldn't. They had one bedroom and Mum and I had the other. Then we had Mrs Loecker and her daughter for a time. They didn't stay long for some reason or another, they moved on. We had the children's home in Ryelands Road, and they took a few evacuees.

Pauline Davies

My father was a headmaster in the Birmingham area so as a child I was an evacuee, and we moved down here during the war to live with my grandparents. Father used to come down at weekends and work as a Special Constable. That was his war work.

Maureen Crumpler

Wartime food

It was short rations right through the war and beyond. My father had a little bit of garden on Perseverance Road. To add to the work in the war years, many people depended a lot on what they produced on their allotments or their garden. They had quite a lot of vegetables during the summer, if the blight and the caterpillars left them alone. In the war years there were no sprays and chemicals available, so that gave Father a lot of work. Every summer there would be a plague of caterpillars, with their insatiable appetites. That meant preparing a bucket of soapsuds and washing the cabbage leaves while they were still growing.

Mervyn Bufton

From the school we had to go out to collect rosehips to make rosehip syrup, foxgloves (very poisonous) to make digitalis, a powerful heart drug. We also collected aluminium and scrap iron which was melted down for the war effort. We were all encouraged to dig our gardens, and keep some poultry to augment our rations.

Stanley Yapp

You had to make the best of everything you could. Because we were on the farm, we were really lucky compared to some people.

We made our own butter, had our own poultry. But food was very scarce and a lot of people didn't have very much.

Elizabeth Lewis

We didn't suffer as much as a lot of people, since my other grandparents had a farm at Hamnish. We had produce from the farm – eggs, and my grandmother used to make butter. It was mostly things like sweets and sugar I can remember being on ration. I think you were allowed an extra ration for preserving, because my grandfather was a very keen gardener and grew a lot of fruit and vegetables.

There was a lot of swapping went on during the war. If you had a glut of something you swapped it for something else. I don't remember a great many shortages. But I was very young and we were brought up with them, so we didn't terribly miss things like sweets, they were just a great treat. We had a sweet tin and you were allowed one sweet a day, provided you behaved! I remember jelly was a great treat which we only had for birthday parties, and blancmange, which I hated. And an iced cake was a great treat for a birthday party.

Maureen Crumpler

The only time I was really aware of the shortages was when we got our sweets. Right opposite our house was Mrs Harrison's sweet and tobacconist's shop, and we used to take our coupons and get a quarter of sweets from her. Apart from that, I don't think we suffered the hardships in Leominster they did in some towns. During the war there was a lot of poaching going on; it was pheasants and ... well, anything really. It was 'fair game', as they say.

Ray Fisher

There were queues for everything. We had very little food – I think it was about four eggs a week my mother had, and about half a pound of butter. We had ration books, and it was nine points for a quarter of sweets, but I used to buy extra points off a friend. We had Mrs Gwilliam's sweet shop next door to us, and I was in and out all the time. Unless you lived on a farm, you had chicken once a year on Christmas Day. We lived on tripe and onions, corned beef and spam, which I've never eaten since. The most popular meat was rabbit – roast or stewed, but always rabbit, all locally caught and sold on the black market.

Pauline Davies

"There were queues for everything."

In the wartime our mother worked miracles, like a good many ladies. Where she got the food from we didn't know, but she never let us go without a dinner of some sort. It would be a stew if she could afford a bit of meat, and of course the dumplings and all the usual things that you would have in a stew. She'd concoct a beautiful stew, but it had to last two or three days.

There was a thing called bacon pieces, the trimmings, and my mother used to send me to Miliases' in West Street, where Dan Walker was the manager. They sold a lot of bacon. My mother said, 'Go and ask for three pennyworths of odds and ends, but don't go in the shop if anyone else is in there! Don't let anyone see you asking for three penn'orth!' That would be the basis of a meal, concocted with something else. The pride was there, but not the money. Lots of people had to do that sort of thing. You always had your pride – the mothers did anyway. We didn't know any different, we were very happy, I remember.

Malcolm Newman

Pigmen frequently visited the streets to collect any left over food for their animals, but little was wasted, so they had a lean time. With meat being rationed and in short supply, like everything else, poachers did a good trade in rabbits, selling them at two shillings and sixpence each. At the same time, enterprising housewives made and sold faggots from their homes, the contents of which were hard to guess at.

Roy Gough

Mother used to have three jam jars on the table and she used to separate it out. You'd have your rations for so long; so much would be put into each jar so that everybody had a fair share. One day my mother came home with some cheese. It was put on the table, and I thought, 'Something's happening here, I can see something moving!' It was absolutely infested with cheese mites. I think that went in the bin!

John Sharp

"I 'ent eating it!"

Oh, queue for this and queue for that. If they had kippers, you'd queue, and then you could only have one. Perhaps just as it came to your turn they'd all have gone. Sid Wright and his son John had a fishmongers shop in Corn Street. We were coming up the street, my neighbour and me, we were pals and would share what we had. Anyhow, this woman said they'd got fish at Sid Wright's, they'd got a big frozen block. She looked at it and said, 'Where do you get your fish from, Mr Wright?' 'From the docks', he said. 'If you want some you can have as much as you like.' She said, 'No thank you. There are dead Germans in there, and I 'ent eating it!'

Margery Hunt

The Ministry of Agriculture seized most of the crop of potatoes, but the small farmers found a way to get round it for both their and their customers' benefit. When the ministry quota had been filled, they instructed that the remainder of the potatoes should be coloured with a purple dye and were only to be used for animal food. However, enterprising farmers sidestepped this instruction and hawked bags of these potatoes around the housing estates, with the customers merely having to peel the outer skin off the potatoes to remove the dye. The farmers thereby had a cash crop and the customers had more food.

Roy Gough

During the war you went out and did different things to help, things you wouldn't have done if it hadn't have been a war. You'd go out and help with the haymaking, and picking fruit, and we had what we called roots, sugar beet. They used to cut the sugar beet and send it off to Kidderminster. I didn't do that work, but the men did.

We had an Italian prisoner of war, two actually. They came at different times and they were put out on the farms, they'd go wherever they were sent. Some of them didn't live in the farmhouse, but the one we had stayed in the house, so he was lucky really. We had Land Army girls helping as well. We had lots of them come and stay on the farm, and some would want to stay on after. There was one young boy, an evacuee from Harwich I think – about sixteen – and he did want to stay, he didn't want to go home.

Elizabeth Lewis

My boss, he got a Land Army girl. They played an important role in the farm work. They were out hoeing and picking up stones off the field into a bucket, then they'd get the bucketful and tip it into the trailer. There'd be thistle bodging to do, dock digging in the corn, and hoeing the sugar beet, then leave it a week or two and then clean any weeds out of it. We had about fifteen acres – that wouldn't be much now, but then it was a fair bit.

Arthur Evans

I was working when the war broke out. I was about thirteen and I spent most of my time on the farm. No pay, we did it all for the love of it, like. There wasn't much money about in those days, by God, there wasn't. Farm wages were only about 30 bob a week or something like that.

George Oakley

During the war years, when it was difficult to get footwear, my father had a useful hand at improvising. There was a shop next door to the Grapes, the pub at the top of Broad Street, which sold leather goods. He used to buy a sheet of leather, and he would repair our shoes until the uppers were so perforated with tacks and seggs that they couldn't take any more. (Seggs were those little metal pieces to put on the toes or on the heels so that they would not wear down so rapidly.) Leather was in such short supply at times that one couldn't buy a sheet of leather, so then Father would just tack on leather in the parts that were most worn down.

Mervyn Bufton

During the war we used to have weeks when people used to be encouraged to put money in National Savings. They used to have

targets – the idea was to put so much money in to buy a Spitfire, or a Corvette. We had 'Wings for Victory' week, 'Warship week', and I think we may have had some other weeks, but I've forgotten. But those were the two main ones.

They used to have something like a temperature gauge showing every day how much had been contributed to National Savings by the local people. They always hit the target. A gentleman in Leominster called Charlie Harvey (he had a clothing business) used to come to the fore and make speeches during this period.

John Sharp

SPITFIRE FUND TOTAL NOW OVER £1900

Success continues to come from the "Bring and Buy" window at Mr C. H. Harvey's premises in Corn Street. Another £20 has been banked this week making £90 in four weeks. In addition to the work which is being done in connection with this window by the Mayoress (Mrs. Hammond), Mrs. J. N. Peatt and others, thanks are due to Mr Harvey for so generously placing the window at the disposal of the Fund.

To-day (Friday) is cabbage plant day at the "Bring and Buy" window. Some hundreds of plants have been given for sale and about 1,000 more bulbs will be offered.

Leominster News Nov 1 1940

Salute the Soldier Week May 6th to 14th 1944. A parade of American and British military units ends in Corn Square

They were raising money for Spitfires. Apparently I was taken to see a Spitfire, or part of a Spitfire that was in the Corn Square. You had to pay whatever it was, half a crown or something, and you could sit in the cockpit, and I was taken to sit in it.

Maureen Crumpler

Blackouts and air raids

You had to have this really dark blackout. The wardens would come round and tell you that there was a crack, you know, showing light. It was terrible to go out in the evening because there was no light at all. It was pitch black. Nowadays you see a light from a house or something, but you couldn't see anything in the blackout. It was frightening.

Dorothy Oughton

The gentleman in charge of ARP for Leominster was Inspector Walters, and he used to live next door to us in Etnam Street. He had a son, and one day his parents were out, and he took me up into his parents' bedroom at the front of the house. He said, 'What do you think of this?' and under the pillow was a revolver. And he started to wave the bloody thing about! I'll tell you straight, I came out of that house like a dose of salts! I didn't want to be shot!

John Sharp

My father was an Air Raid Warden, and he used to have to go out at night on patrol. The German bombers droned overhead, with many searchlights shining up into the night sky. My sister and I were very frightened, and we used to take the dog in the house.

Stanley Yapp

Bargy Hughes was the Air Raid Warden for the area round where he lived in the Crescent. You'd be asleep in bed, and he'd come round, and he'd tap on the bedroom window, and say 'Warning out, air raid warning out'.

Margery Hunt

The blackout is the thing I remember the most. Everything was black. We all felt very safe with the soldiers, we could go out and walk around and there was no fear.

Pauline Davies

Sometimes when we'd been out at night, coming home, I used to count the gates until I got to my own place, because there were no lights. The windows were blacked out.

Phyllis Manson

I was an Air Raid Warden, along with my father and my brother, who was a messenger boy. Mum stayed at home and looked after the house and the shop.

Our offices were over in what was Cooper's, the solicitors in West Street. We used to sign on there, and then Dad and I were allocated Vicarage Street. Where I'm living now was the air raid shelter, and this is where we used to come and open doors in case it was needed.

Minnie Davies

I can remember the air raid shelter in Vicarage Street. We used to play in it, and it was as dark as anything in there! The front of it is still there, but it's part of a bungalow now.

Ray Watkins

Leominster Air Raid Precautions 1944
The ARP helped with rescue and was responsible for the handing out of gas masks, the upkeep of local public shelters, and the maintenance of the blackout.
Bryan Davies is on the left, Minnie Davies behind Harley Davies Junior, and Harley Davies in front of the air raid shelter in Vicarage Street

I suppose it was a gradual process, but I can remember when my dad was called up. All my friends' dads were called up, and it just seemed a natural thing. He didn't get called up till 1943. He was 41 or so, and went in the Royal Pioneer Corps. His apprentices, Fred and Jim, were both called up as well, so that was that. Fred and Jim were only eighteen or nineteen then.

Ray Fisher

During the war many Leominster people worked at the munitions factory at Rotherwas, Hereford, and travelled to work by a special diesel railcar from Leominster station. In July 1942 a German raider bombed the factory, killing scores of workers. On the day of the raid I remember seeing workers coming off the train in late afternoon and walking up Etnam Street in a dazed and dishevelled state. It must have been a great shock to them. I was told that the plane was flying so low that you could see the aircrew.

John Sharp

My mother worked down at the ammunition factory in Hereford. About five o'clock in the morning they used to go down to the station on the mail. She was there when the bus overturned on Dinmore, and she was there when bombs were dropped. I don't know a great deal about what happened – obviously she wasn't one of the casualties – but there were quite a few killed down there.

Pauline Davies

My brother was called up, well, both my brothers were, but the other one failed. They said his hearing wasn't 100%, so they couldn't pass him for the army, and he went down the pits, which to my idea was worse.

My mother was in the munition factory at Rotherwas, and her hair turned orange at the front. I shall never forget it! They had to wear scarves over their heads, but the explosives must have made their hair go orange.

Dorothy Oughton

Leominster Observer Corps at The Rugg.
On steps: bottom: F. Lewis (in hat), above: F. Williams
On platform: ?
Front left to right: ? Freeman (The Oak), ? Birch, ? Heyward,
G.B. Lloyd, ? Smith (in Beret), H. Slaymaker (wearing hat),
W.G. Beaman, ? Harrison (at rear), F.A. Daley, ? Spurrier, J. Smith
(with white hair), R.G. Preece, Carwardine, J. Thompson

Apart from the siren being tested every day, I think it may have been at twelve or one o'clock, we didn't hear anything. As a child at Newlands I remember lying in bed and hearing the sound of bombers going overhead, with this peculiar droning noise. Wave after wave of them, and although it didn't mean a lot to me, my father would say the next day, 'They were bombing Liverpool again last night'. We heard them coming as they flew up over this side of the country.

Once we heard a plane coming over very low. We all rushed outside to see what it was, and as it came over the farmhouse my father suddenly realised that it didn't have British markings, but German. So we all rushed back inside very rapidly, and about ten minutes later a couple of Spitfires came over, presumably having been alerted.

Maureen Crumpler

The siren in Leominster was at the rear of Woolworth's, and my bedroom window was within yards of it. It used to go off all the time and it was very noisy! Whenever there were any signs of anything happening, it went off.

Pauline Davies

Being in such a remote area, the war was far away. But the first time the air raid siren went, both my brother and myself, we trembled. We thought that after the siren went, we could expect bombing. The first night that the Germans made for Liverpool, following the line of the railway, we heard the air raid siren give the warning, and then came the thunder of the planes. Of course they didn't fly so very high in those days, and they flew very slowly by our reckoning. It would take a long time between hearing the sound and then its total departure – it could be ten or fifteen minutes. The first time we heard the air raid warning followed by the sound of enemy aircraft passing overhead we went into our shelter under the stairs, and of course we were very relieved when later we heard the all-clear. I suppose people nowadays would not be able to sense the difference that there was between the alert sound and the all-clear sound. The alert – oh! it sort of throws up the stomach – O-O-O-O-O-O. The all-clear is a smooth sound, it's so calming. We got used to the siren, though, because Liverpool was bombed on nine consecutive nights.

Mervyn Bufton

"All of a sudden we both went up in the air!"

The winter of 1940/41 was the period of the Blitz over Britain. The German bombers were flying over regularly, crossing Herefordshire going up to Liverpool. First of all the siren would go, then you would hear the drone – woom-woom-woom – and they would pass over. Many a night we were disturbed by the air raid siren and the menacing throb of the bombers' engines overhead. But this one particular night the siren had gone, and I don't think we'd gone to bed. We were all downstairs, and heard this plane going over, and suddenly we heard an almighty explosion which shook the house. The pilot of one of the planes must have decided to drop his bombs and head for home. To think the ruddy Germans could do that!

Our evacuee, Len Baxter, threw himself under the table – he had experienced air raids in London. The rest of the family just sat there in shock with looks of disbelief. We thought at the time that the town had been hit and people killed. The following morning we were told that the bombs had missed the town but had landed in a field on the left-hand side of the Ludlow road just beyond the railway crossing. So off we went to see. There were quite deep craters, and there was the stench of cordite, a kind of sickly smell, and shrapnel all over the place. I think one cow was killed. We were going in and out, poking around looking for shrapnel. Really there should have been a policeman on duty, stopping people going into the field. There could have had an unexploded bomb which could have gone off later, but no, we were just in the field poking around, exploring.

John Sharp

Once I was up the street and some of us women were stood talking when all of a sudden the siren went and we very nearly jumped out of our skins. They'd say 'Take cover', but we never bothered.

We only had one lot of bombs, right opposite where we lived. My husband was home on leave at the time – good job he was, because it did frighten me half to death. We were in bed, and all of a sudden we both went up in the air! My neighbour downstairs, her husband had just come home that night and they hadn't gone to bed yet, they were having a cup of tea. They were sat one each side of the fire, and she said the cups went out of their hands, and they went up in the air and back down again.

There was some gypsies opposite us in a caravan, with a river running in front of them, and one of them said, 'I thought we was going to end up in the river! Our caravan went up in the air!'

Margery Hunt

When they had those bombs dropped in Leominster, I was in Pembridge with my gran. She went to the door because we'd heard the bang. Everything seemed to shake in Pembridge, we heard the noise up there, and it's eight miles away. My grandad said 'Oh, it's only the wind down the chimney.' Gran went to the door, and there was a policeman who used to walk up and down. He said, 'They've bombed the Clifton.' Granny started crying then: 'Oh, all those kids, they'll be hurt.' Anyway, she went back out again and somebody else came down and said it was the hospital! That was even worse. It was about three days before we heard that it was just the cows that had been killed. There were no phones or anything to get in touch then. She was frightened, my gran was, and nothing would calm her, nothing, until she knew.

Dorothy Oughton

One night, looking eastwards from the steps at the end of Perseverance Road, the sky in the far distance was an orange glow. It seemed to be oscillating, like flames. But at a distance one couldn't be sure. Someone there on those steps said it could be as far away as Worcester. We couldn't hear anything. What could it be? Was it some great arms dump or petroleum dump? We couldn't figure it out, but it looked awful, a sight never seen before. The next day we learned that it was the awful night when Coventry was rained with incendiary bombs, and Coventry, as the crow flies, is approximately fifty miles away.

Mervyn Bufton

Walter Parris, who used to run the greengrocer's shop just at the back where Parry's Greengrocer is now, told me that in the war he was in the local fire brigade, and they used to get called out to go

The wartime National Fire Service in Leominster. Only one of this group has been identified, Dennis Hemmingway, standing third from the right

to Coventry when the bombing was on. They'd travel all the way to Coventry on an open-topped fire engine, and they were so cold when they got there ... they used to be absolutely frozen.

Ray Watkins

One sad event at the height of the war concerned the horse that pulled the railway parcel van. On the day of the accident the van was parked outside Ross's shop in the High Street. Unfortunately, an army lorry struck the rear of the van when passing. The horse was lifted by the shafts of the van and propelled through the shop's plate glass window, landing on the display decking, which collapsed, dropping the poor animal into the cellar. Nothing could be done for the horse other than calling a vet to put it out of its misery. Many of the local people who witnessed this event were moved to tears over the death of this poor animal.

John Sharp

Tommies and GIs

The Army moves in

Leominster was full of troops; there were troops everywhere, whole battalions of them. We'd have them to tea; they'd come to the farm, and we'd have them for the afternoon.

Elizabeth Lewis

The army requisitioned many of the larger buildings in the town for accommodation. The officers' mess was at the Waverley Hotel in Etnam Street, now the site of a nursing home. The large Georgian houses at 20 and 22 Etnam Street were used as a barracks and headquarters – one had a sentry box outside – and the old cinema on Corn Square became the Navy, Army and Air Force Institute Canteen (NAAFI).

The area of the town over the bridge and the Easters, bordering the River Lugg and running up to Eaton Hill, including the Rifle Butts, was the training area where the army carried out exercises. These fields were still open to the public, but they were closed when red flags were flying, warning of firing or exercises. Some days there was great activity, with rifle, machine gun and mortar firing. Exercises would go on through the night, with explosions and flares lighting up the sky. After an exercise the area would be searched for unexploded mortar bombs and flares. Unfortunately, after one exercise, two young boys from the town found an unexploded flare and started to throw it to one another. One of the boys caught it, the flare ignited, and he was seriously injured.

John Sharp

I remember seeing galvanised huts in the fields behind the hedges, probably ten to fifteen yards apart. There'd be four or five in a field along the hedge, rather like large chicken coops. They were made of galvanised iron and they were absolutely full of metal ammunition boxes. I don't know why they were there, but I remember being told that that's what was in them.

Maureen Crumpler

There were troops billeted all the time. There were the Hallamshires and various other regiments. Etnam Street had the most billets. Waverley House, Abbeyfield, the houses up the steps were used as well, and so was Faulkner House, which was demolished in the 50s or 60s, and the Bateman Buildings round the back of the Westbury. That was absolutely loaded with English soldiers. They'd go round into the Square and get their fish and chips. They

135

caused no problems; they were very nice and very helpful. When my mother would allow it, we used to take their dogs for a walk. One of them, Jim, left his dog with me when they left.

Pauline Davies

"We had no idea where we were going."

We boarded the train at Gourock. It was crammed full! We had no idea where we were going – hadn't a clue! Anyhow, we were given sandwiches to last us for the journey and managed to get a drink from somewhere as we travelled through the night. We kept stopping in sidings, half an hour here, an hour there, but eventually we arrived in the early morning at a small market town called Leominster in Herefordshire. We stepped from the train and were told to leave our kitbags in a pile at the station, and then we marched to our billets about half a mile away. We were in civilian houses on the streets of the town. They were mostly big, rambling, Victorian-type houses, and all the furniture had been taken out, leaving just the bare floor boards and blackout frames in the windows.

Arthur Green of the Hallamshire Battalion

A few of us went into this pub, and there were quite a few chaps in there, and we said, 'We're new to Leominster. What do you drink here?' We knew it was cider country and we started off with this stuff, and it was pints all round. We later left the pub and went across the road to our accommodation, where the whole lot of us passed out.

Ivor Slater of the Hallamshire Battalion

My father got to know some of the Hallamshire Regiment because of the chapel he went to. They opened a rest centre for soldiers in the town several nights a week. They provided writing materials for writing a letter to send to a wife or relative, and the good folk served a cup of tea.

Mervyn Bufton

When one of our evacuees moved out, the army commandeered the front bedroom and living room as an officer's billet. So at that time our small three-bedroomed terraced house accommodated a family of three, an evacuee, and an officer plus his batman during the day. Our officer was 2nd Lieutenant Palmer; I understand he was from the 'Huntley and Palmer' family. He was a very, very nice gentleman. Many a night he decided to stay with the family and play board games with Len Baxter and the other boys from the school rather than go up to the mess. When you took an officer in you also took in his batman, and his was called Billiard. He used to arrive first thing in the morning to polish the officer's boots and prepare his shaving water. Billiard was an old soldier, an old regular. He'd served on the Northwest Frontier, and he was a real character, a nice man to talk to. I remember we went sledging on the hill one winter, and Palmer came with us. Billiard came along, but he couldn't walk with us, because he couldn't walk with the officer.

John Sharp

Sometimes the troops trained on the children's playground at the Grange. It was quite open in the war years, and there was a firing range with live ammunition on the flank of Eaton Hill. It's now been filled in and smoothed out, there's no sign of it. So troops would come to the firing range for firing practice, and drill practice on the children's playing field. There was one unhappy incident when the troops were going through firing drill. They weren't meant to have live ammunition, but someone had a live round in his rifle. Of course, when you shoulder the rifle, you take aim at something. He took aim at a child, and the child was killed.

Mervyn Bufton

We were down there with him. There were about six of us from Croft Street, and we all used to play together, boys and girls. There was Mabel, who was a cousin to this boy, Dick Price, and there was his brother. We were waiting for him to come down from the slide, and he did come down, but he'd been shot. It was awful, awful. His brother went berserk. They shouldn't have been using ordinary bullets anyway – they were supposed to have been blanks – and he shouldn't have been firing towards us at all. He should have been firing towards the target.

Dorothy Oughton

There was a woman shot and killed in Leominster. Her name was Mrs Ree. I remember hearing it as a child, when I wasn't supposed to be listening. My mother knew her; she worked down at the ammunition factory in Rotherwas, and she called for my mother on the way down. She was having an affair with a British soldier, a Sergeant Bullock, they had a big argument, and he shot her by Bateman's Building. He served a long time in prison. It was a very big thing at the time, a nationwide scandal.

Pauline Davies

The Americans

The Americans' presence was very visible. They came to Leominster in 1943, a year before D-Day, in large numbers. They had billets in fields to the right of Green Lane, and at the bottom of the Bargates.

Mervyn Bufton

These two American officers arrived on the scene. They came to see my father and wanted to know if they could buy fresh fruit from him. I thought they were so smart. Their uniforms were so smart. They seemed to settle into the town extremely well.

John Sharp

Barons Cross Camp was an American hospital. They had proper operating theatres there and everything; it was quite a big camp. They employed electricians, carpenters and plumbers, and men who kept the boilers going all the time for the heating and water for the operating theatres, that sort of thing. My father worked there. He also worked at Ashfield, now the nursing home at the top of the Bargates.

Ray Watkins

The first hospital train arrived at Leominster station within a few days of D-Day. A fleet of about forty ambulances were waiting to unload the casualties, who were taken through the town to the hospital. After an interval of about half an hour a few ambulances returned to the station to collect those who had died in transit. Every few days this procedure would be repeated until the successful breakout from the Normandy beachhead.

John Sharp

They came in convoys up Etnam Street to the camp at Barons Cross, and all of us children used to get up and look out of our bedroom windows at them, 'cos we weren't allowed on the street when there was a load coming in. It was the same with the gypsies when they used to come up Etnam Street, we had to be in then as well.

Pauline Davies

There were quite a lot of Polish people in the town in the war. In fact, when we moved out to Bargates my grandfather let the house part of the shop in the High Street to a Polish family who were there for quite a long time. There were also people from the American airforce at the hospital who would come and visit various houses when they were well enough to walk about. There was an 'Adopt an Airman' scheme, I think, and they would come and have tea and be entertained by the

families. One or sometimes two would come to tea, and bring us sweets – beautiful fondants which unfortunately tasted of soap, possibly because they came in with a consignment of soap, but were nevertheless greatly appreciated. Sweets were on ration, of course, at that time.

Maureen Crumpler

I didn't mind the Polish soldiers, but I just couldn't bear the Yanks. The Polish ones, we used to go to the dances with them. They were different altogether, you know, quite polite and different. But I didn't think the Americans were very nice; I didn't like them at all, for some reason.

Eileen Bacon

When our soldiers came home on leave there was a lot of jealousy over the Americans. There was quite a lot of that, but saying that, they were excellent to the children, they were wonderful. They had female soldiers as well. They took all the children to Barons Cross camp and it was the first time we'd ever tasted gateau. To us it was absolutely marvellous; we only had about two eggs a week, and about half a pound of sugar. They used to walk round the town in twos and we used to pester them for gum: 'Any gum chum?' There was another sweet which I've never seen since; they called it Soap-dope, it was like a red chewing gum. It didn't taste very special but it was sweet, and you only had nine points of sweets a month.

Pauline Davies

I remember the Americans coming through Dilwyn in lorries and throwing sweets. I can still taste them; I can't describe the taste, but I can still taste it. It was so ... well, we didn't have things like that.

Lee McColgan

The first American units which came to Leominster were well behaved. Their Military Police, called 'Snowdrops' because of their white helmets, were armed with baseball bats and would stand no nonsense if anyone misbehaved. I suppose these units were changing all the time as part of the build-up for the second front. They all dressed the same, with no distinguishing flashes or badges, unlike the British troops. This changed near D-Day, when a Ranger Battalion (the equivalent to the British Commandoes) became the garrison battalion. At the same time, an American negro transport battalion was billeted just outside the town. In order to prevent fights between the men, the two battalions were barred from being in town at the same time in the evening. However, this did not prevent fights occurring and I understand that one white soldier was stabbed to death outside the Clifton cinema. I also witnessed a nasty brawl outside the White Lion at the bottom of Etnam Street late one evening.

John Sharp

The main problem was that when the Americans were here, it became common to see condoms lying around everywhere. It didn't exactly boost our confidence in them! Obviously their interest was mainly in the womenfolk of Leominster.

Only occasionally did one get into a chat with an American. They would have a guard outside the exit from their quarters in Bargates, and being an American guard you could chat with

him, not like a British guard on sentry duty. I can recall one conversation. One of us said, 'What do you think of the blacks?' 'Oh', he said, 'I'd like to stick this bayonet right through them all!' They were segregated; there were areas for whites only and areas for blacks only.

Mervyn Bufton

I was walking down South Street once to go and meet my friends, to go to the pictures, when I thought I'd bumped into a lamppost. All of a sudden it said 'Sorry'! I looked up and all I could see was the whites of his eyes. Oh, it frightened me, I thought I'd bumped into a lamppost, but he was a black soldier. They were treated terribly.

Dorothy Oughton

You'd only see the Americans when you came in to market on a Friday. I wasn't very pleased with them sometimes, the way they treated black soldiers from their own country. The black soldiers were made to walk on the street when they saw the white soldiers coming, step down off the pavement and stand on the street while they passed. I thought it was awful. Of course it altered after the war. They couldn't go on doing that, could they? A good job too. It was an awful way to treat another man, terrible. I couldn't bear to see it. I felt like telling them off, but I knew that would be no good.

Elizabeth Lewis

I used to serve in the fish and chip shop next to the Three Horseshoes in Corn Square. One day I went to serve this black person who was sitting there, and these white men started saying that they should have priority. I told them that this other man was there before them, and it was his turn to be served. The manager asked what the matter was, I told him, and he told me not to worry, as I was only doing what I thought was right. They were grumbling because I went and took his order first, but the manager took no notice of them.

Phyllis Manson

Things did get nasty towards the end. There was a negro battalion, transport drivers, based somewhere on the outskirts of the town, and then there were Americans Rangers. They had orders not to be in town off duty at night at the same time, but things did happen. I know there was a rumpus at the bottom of Etnam Street, a hell of a fight. I heard it, actually – I was in the house on my own and I heard all this terrible noise going on outside. It was a very nasty punch-up between the two different types of Americans. I understand that one of the white Americans got knifed outside the Clifton cinema.

John Sharp

During the war we used to have a dance down at the 'Stute. We used to go down there once a week. If the white Yanks were in the dance hall, the blacks couldn't go in. Then we had a fair down by the station. These white Yanks were on the dodgem cars, and this one black soldier got on there and he stabbed this white bloke. They all ran up and stood outside the 'Stute. A friend of mine lived nearby, and we went into her house and watched. They threw their knives into the road, and nobody would say whose knife it was, so they never found out who did it.

Dorothy Oughton

Victory

The Americans held a party at Batemans Buildings for all the local kids on VE Day. They had lemonade and cakes – the usual kids' stuff. The Americans were very good, actually.

Ray Fisher

I can remember going down to the Corn Square in Leominster on VE Day. People were singing and dancing, and the bells were ringing; there was huge hilarity, and we danced the hokey-cokey in the Square.

Was it on VE or VJ Day the Americans threw a party for all the children in the town at Batemans Buildings? We had a procession of the children from the infant school, and possibly the juniors in fancy dress. There's a photograph of myself and Judith Lee Thomas leading the procession with Mrs Maddox the headmistress. We all processed to Batemans Buildings where we had a party – sandwiches, jelly and then cake at the end, if you were nicely brought up, like I was. There was a little boy sitting opposite us who hadn't heard of this regulation, so he started straight in to the cakes, much to our disgust, because we'd got our eye on them. He ate all the fancy tops off the cakes, and left all the bottom bits for us!

Maureen Crumpler

There was a street party the day the war ended, probably VJ Day. It was the whole length of Etnam Street. It joined up with the Worcester Road residents and their party. I can't think how many people were there. We had a competition, and Mrs Gillam, who had the sweetshop, had made me this outfit. I had a man's black suit with a bowler hat and it had struck matches sewn onto it, as there was a match strike at the time. We had trestle tables all the

Maureen Davies, Judith Lee Thomas and infant school headmistress Mrs Maddox lead the parade

VE Day celebrations May 1945. All children between 5 and 14 were invited to a special performance at the Clifton Cinema followed by a party at the New Exchange. The children called the soldier in the photograph 'Blue-eyes'. To his right is Beryl Hicks in a dark cardigan. Robert Fairbanks is on the far right with the glasses, Peter England in the dark jacket is immediately behind him

way down the street, and the food was good. All the women got together and made sandwiches, jellies, all that kind of thing. There was dancing all night. They really went to town, it was wonderful.

Pauline Davies

We had a street party in Hampton Gardens on VE Day. There were about twenty children there – something like that. There would have been rationing, but there didn't seem to be a shortage of food, not as far as I can remember. Vicarage Street had a party the same day. I can remember their trestles at the far end of Vicarage Street, and we were up the top end of Hampton Gardens.

Ray Watkins

With the war in Europe over on the 8th of May 1945, the people of the town celebrated VE Day with street parties and dancing in the Grange. During the celebrations athletics were held and I was lucky to win the 100 and 220 yards sprints. After the celebrations the Americans welcomed the townspeople to a barbecue and sports at Eaton Hill House, where they introduced us to the game of baseball and all its complications!

On VJ Day I was visiting relatives in Scotland. I travelled down from Glasgow to Leominster by train on the night of the national celebrations, and witnessed the beacons lit by the towns and villages lighting up the night sky for miles around.

John Sharp

I went up to London after the war; they had holes in the roads where they had had great big bonfires. It was a terrible war, and the end of it was a wonderful time.

Pauline Davies

The Children's Fancy Dress Carnival VJ Day 1945 after the presentation of prizes at the New Exchange Building. The entries in the Carnival were so numerous that it took some time for the procession to move around Westbury and on to the Grange

Perseverance Road and Bargates VJ Day street party

Some of the organisers of the Perseverance Road and Bargates VJ party. Far left, Mrs Matthews. Adjusting character's hat, Mrs Julian. With jug, Mrs Hackett. Next to Mrs Hackett, from left to right: Mrs Daws, Mrs Fletcher, Letty Harris, Mrs Strangward. At rear, Mrs Jarvis, Mary Gibbs, Mrs Pritchard, Mrs Greenhouse, Mrs Morgan (with glasses)

Part Three
Post-war Leominster

As the troops returned after the war to find work and pick up the threads of their lives, Leominster started a vast programme of building. Older 'decayed' houses were swept away and construction started on the large estates at Cranes Lane, Churchill Avenue, the Sandpits and Westfield.

Although many still found employment providing services for the community, there were now more jobs in manufacturing. Factories such as Cadburys at Marlbrook, Hawkins Paper and Plastics, Delson and Son, Lambourns of Westbury Street, Dent and Allcroft Gloves and Oakleigh Animal Products, provided hundreds of jobs. While in construction the agricultural engineers F.H. Dale of Mill Street, and Ernest Mifflin of Worcester Road, together with builders G. Morris of New Street and G.P. Thomas of Green Lane flourished. There was plenty of work to go round.

Even as the town expanded it still took some time to tackle long-standing problems. The seemingly inevitable floods of the Lugg and Kenwater in Bridge and Mill Streets were not finally solved until the 1960s and traffic congestion was eventually eased by the building of an inner relief road, and later a long-awaited bypass in 1988.

The town was changing, and these final extracts record this. But they also echo some of the stories from the earlier generations. They are a reassuring reminder that some things do not change.

Back to work

When I came back from the army I went to see about getting my job back, but the owner had just been demobbed, and there was no business. My mother used to deal with a grocer's shop, Barber and Manuel, in Gaunt street. The boss, Mr Barber, used to give me a biscuit when I was a boy and he worked for Burtons the grocers. He offered me a room above the greengrocer's shop to start up on my own, and to cut a long story short I started up there. I met another fellow I used to work with before the war; he was a barber too, so we started together. We were up there for some years before we bought a shop in Drapers Lane.

Fred Parsons

My father didn't talk about it much because he was part of the 'forgotten army'. When he came out of the army, there was only Mum there at the station. He was quite ashamed that nobody else met him.

Meryl Boff

I was called up six days before my eighteenth birthday, and when I was demobbed in 1947 I was really pleased to get back to Leominster. After having about three weeks off I went back to driving round the farms picking up churns of milk for Cadbury's.

It changed from churns into tankers, and then the lorries got bigger, and I went on to tankers taking milk down to London. I'd be there at five o'clock in the morning – Willesden, Palmers Green, Cricklewood, Battersea, Manor Park, places like that. Then I went on to artics, hauling chocolate in the rough like to different dairies. I enjoyed lorry driving. Liverpool, Leicester, Peterborough, Northampton, Luton – we used to go to all those places.

Ronald Cooke

My father came back to settle in Leominster after the war, but the employment situation was dreadful, and the wages were terrible. He was going to go to Cadbury's, but he ended up working for Joseph Lucas in Birmingham, and he came home at the weekends. The money was almost double that in Leominster.

Pauline Davies

After I was demobilised after the war, because I'd done a lot of engineering work on tanks, I worked for a garage in Bridge Street and I was there about five years. My wages in those days were £5 10 shillings a week; that was a good wage in those days. I used to give it all to my wife because I could get tips. People would ask you to bring their car out, run you back, and give you half a crown. So I could make do without stopping anything out of my wages.

There was rationing, and of course there was a great black market. A farmer from six miles out came to my boss and offered him a salted bacon pig. My boss didn't want that, he only wanted a piece, and he had a terrific argument. In fact, that farmer never came to us for petrol afterwards.

Alec Haines

I liked school but I loved farming. At the end of the war the young farmers started coming back to the little villages and having competitions. George Lewis had a Matchless Motorcycle 350. I'd put my hoe under my arm and get on the bike and hang on to him for grim death, and we would go round to lots of these places for beet-hoeing competitions. You had to do eight rows, twenty-five yards. I used to win a lot of competitions then, because I was pretty good at it. Then I started working at Woodhampton Farm. After I'd been there for three years, the bailiff left and Mr Gardner offered me the job on the farm. I was there for twenty-five years, and I managed the farm at the finish. I was very interested in Pedigree Herefords. They sold as bloodstock and the cattle went all over the country, or abroad to Ireland and European countries. I went to Smithfield in London several times, but we never entered cattle there, we wanted to see what was showing and selling. My very best day was one time at Hereford Market. There was about 350 bulls there, and they were judged one day and sold the next. I took third prize with one bull. The champion sold for 250 guineas, but mine was such a good bull that he sold for 800 guineas.

George Oakley

The summer I took the School Certificate I sought an interview with the local surveyor, and he said he'd most likely take me on as a pupil. I got my School Cert. but by then the surveyor had resigned from the Council, so I was left high and dry. I went back to school and continued in the Sixth Form until I was called up for National Service at Christmas.

When I came home after National Service I was introduced to Mr Smith, the sanitary inspector. He said he would take me on, but I would not receive any payment from the Council. I was extremely lucky to qualify for an ex-serviceman's grant – it was a Further Education and Training Scheme. I had maintenance for one year, and travelling expenses, course fees, the lot.

John Sharp

"It was very, very boring ..."

I left school at fifteen and I wanted to go to Peggy Morrows, an old-fashioned hairdresser that used to be down Drapers Lane. But in those days you had to pay the hairdresser to be trained, and you had to buy your own equipment. I can remember exactly how much it was; you had to pay the hairdresser 12/6d a week. With the lost wage as well it would have cost over £3 – well, my parents couldn't afford that. So I went into Dents glove factory on South Street. I worked there for about two years, though I didn't like the job very much. The gloves were already cut out and you sewed them together using a tiny machine. I got paid £2 2s, a week, and with piecework I could earn up to £2 17/6d a week. It was very, very boring, but in those days that's what you had to do – whatever job was available, really.

Meryl Boff

I retired from the RAF and got a job with the Post Office in Leominster. I didn't find out until years later that it was the Forces Retirement Officer who got me the job. There were two deliveries in those days to pre-war places. Places built since the war didn't get a second delivery, except in the town. Some of the town rounds would be walking, and then you'd have to cycle with the second round. With the Post Office, it was a five o'clock start, half past four for Christmas pressure. I still get up at five o'clock today. If you worked a through shift you finished at two o'clock. If you were on a split shift, you'd work from five till ten, and then you was back in the afternoon from two till six. I didn't find it easy. My first training was on South Street, Hereford Road and Churchill Avenue with Charlie Childs, then with Harold Thomas on Hope-under-Dinmore in preparation for doing the first part of the Hope round over the Christmas period. That first Christmas it was half past four in the morning, often till nine or ten at night, a good overtime docket.

Herbert Millichamp

I had a job before I left school, at Greenlands of Hereford, where Marks and Spencer's is now. It was a wonderful store, like a mini Harrods. I worked in the hat department, and I got 29/6d a week, which I suppose was adequate then. My bus fare was 1/1d a day, so that really was awful, because I only took home about 22 shillings a week. I wasn't home until three o'clock on a Thursday afternoon, which was my half day, and we had to work all day Saturday.

After that, three of us went from Leominster to Ping's College of Hereford for about a year, and got all our exams in shorthand, typing, and bookkeeping. The first job that came along was only a temporary job; it was at the bookmakers at the rear of Drapers Lane. The wages were about £3. It was considered quite a good job then. Vic Nichols ran it and we had about four runners who brought in most of the bets, and we also took them over the counter. I absolutely loved it! It was exciting, that was the part I liked about it, it wasn't dull. I was there in 1953, the Coronation year when Pinza won the Derby. But when it was over the sticks, Vic didn't want to know, so it was really a seasonal job, and I left.

Then I went to the dentist as a nurse. We had to answer the door, make appointments and stand by the dentist mixing the fillings and all the rest of it. The National Health Service had just come in, and the dental surgeon, Charles Houseman, hated it with a vengeance. He mostly had private patients. Our stamp then for the National Health was threepence, it was a great scheme, there's no doubt about that. I mean, people actually came and had dentistry and dentures, which they couldn't have afforded if it hadn't been for the National Health Service. There was a great shortage of dentists, they couldn't get them for love nor money. I think most of them were probably in private practice as well.

Pauline Davies

I was offered the job of maintenance fitter at the gas works, in the 1950s, which increased my wages tremendously. I was five and a half years at Leominster, and then Tenbury Gas Works came under Leominster, and I was appointed foreman for both places. We had to clean out these great big pipes. They had what they called an auger, that's a screw thing with a length of rod; it would be sixteen foot, at least. You had to get this up the pipe and push it up to get the tar out. Then the chemist who came from Birmingham and tested everything, and I was told I was producing far more gas per ton of coal than had ever been done before.

"For the life of me, I don't know how I survived."

Safety was the main thing about making gas. I would have charts which I had to look at several times a day in case something was building up. There was an awful lot of maintenance and I had gauges, you know, to show the pressures, so if anything looked serious, I could deal with it. I had a good lot of labourers there, and we had two lorries and an old tractor, and a van.

When we turned to North Sea gas everyone had to have a new attachment. Some of these poor old folks had very, very old cookers, almost came from the Ark, you might say. They couldn't have this attachment, so these poor people had to buy another gas cooker. They'd buy second-hand because they couldn't afford new ones.

The gas works closed and Sydney Hinton bought the site, and later he sold it to the Borough Council for exactly the same price that he bought it for. Parts of the plant was just cemented in, and some of the large machinery is still under the ground.

It was a great industry, but for the life of me, I don't know how I survived. I was working in unclean gas before it had gone through the processes, more or less raw gas. If there was a problem, I'd be working in that – we didn't have masks like they have today. You just carried on. Perhaps that's the reason I'm talking to you now, a few weeks off being eighty-eight – perhaps it had a good effect on me, I don't know!

Alec Haines

The last load of coke to be delivered to the Leominster gasworks in March 1960

Pearl Assurance had an office at the top of Broad Street, and one of the Pearl agents told me a chap was leaving, so I took over his book. I had on my book, and I'm now talking about the 1950s, policies for a ha'penny. I didn't go and see the person each week; I'd collect two shillings and tuppence a year. I did well, especially with farmers, because I knew them all. I enjoyed Pearl Insurance and they treated me very well, I must say. I worked for them for twenty-one years.

Alec Haines

I was at Lambourns for ten years. They did powder puffs, hand and arm bands, and they sewed braces and suspenders for gents. Then they had what they called the cresting section, which did enamelling, making cuff-links and tie pins and that. It was all done by hand by just ordinary girls like me, and fired. You went in and were taught what to do, how to mix the mixtures to put in the receptacles.

Miss Wheeler was in charge of the girls doing the powder puffs. I went in to help her, and to inspect the sewing when it was done, checking the items as they came in.

Minnie Davies

I went to Switchgear, down the bottom of Worcester Road; we used to wire components for Herberts of Coventry. I worked from half past seven in the morning until five o'clock. I went from £2 17s 6d to about £8 a week, and that was big money in those days.

Everybody stares at you on your first day, and it was quite daunting seeing all those faces turn round and look at me. But once the first week was over I was fine. I knew everybody,

the Mifflins were all down there, and people from around the Crescent, because it was within walking distance.

There must have been about fifty girls in my section, rows of girls with different machines, doing things like putting a nut and bolt into two pieces of metal that went in my cabinet. Then it was all put together, and all I did was put the wires in. There were grommets which I threaded the wires through, following a chart. In the end you could do it without looking at the chart. I had two hours to complete this job; it was piece work. They had to be taped together to make them neat and tidy, you couldn't have them any old how, and then they were inspected.

"There was no health and safety, good heavens no."

The lorries brought sheets of metal in, held with bands. When I'd been there quite a while, one day some of the bands must have snapped and the sheets of metal went down the factory like a pack of cards. Everybody was jumping out the way, and the noise was horrendous! Luckily nobody was hurt. There was no health and safety, good heavens no. I used to put the rubbers round these casings with trichloroethylene; that's a banned substance today. There was all the noise, the banging, and we had an open spray booth. But everyone was glad of the money; people used to beg for overtime. Everybody seemed happy down there; it was a nice place to work.

When I got married the whole factory collected for me, they collected £22. That was a lot of money! I was quite choked that they had all collected for me, being so young, you know.

I stayed there until it closed down in about 1970. I was heartbroken. Because I'd been there so long, I was one of the last ones to leave. I think about 250 people lost their jobs. We had redundancy pay, but it was hard for most people.

Meryl Boff

In those days, if banks had surplus cash they would send it in a parcel to their head office in London. It was called an HVP – High Value Packet. They were passed hand-to-hand and there was a special book to enter them in. In fact, we lost an HVP from Leominster in the Great Train Robbery in 1963 – the Midland Bank, they'd sent one. I remember saying to the chap that sent it, 'A bit of history here – that's one you sent that never got to the other end!'

Doug Lewis

I came into Leominster to the factory, off Dishley Street. All the stuff went to pet foods. It was the best job I ever had. I wished I'd gone there years earlier. It was very good money, and the overtime was very good.

The lorries would go round the slaughterhouses and bring back any sort of meat. We used to have no end of stuff from Sun Valley [Hereford]. The lorries would come in at the top end,

where the four freezers was. They'd unload it there. Mostly it was in bins; you had to roll them to the back of the lorry, and a forklift would bring them in. My job was helping unload. There was another chap there washing the bins, and then we had to throw them back on the lorry. We'd do seven or eight lorries like that.

It would be all pulped up; you wouldn't have a clue what it was at the end. There were two blokes down that end on machines, it would go in a big bin and then it was refined. Then they used to take it back up to the freezer.

I was there about ten years, but it ended sadly because we were all made redundant.

Arthur Evans

"I always carried a hatpin ..."

I went to work for Yeomans Motors in Hereford, in the booking office. I'd go in on the Midland Red bus and come back on the Yeomans when I did mornings. I'd go in on the Yeomans and come back on the last bus from Hereford, the Midland Red at half past ten, when I did afternoons.

On some nights I couldn't bank the money or get any of the drivers or conductors to bank it for me up in High Town, so I used to bring it home with me in a deposit bag. It would vary from £30 or £40 to several hundred pounds. So I always carried a hatpin. When I got to the corner of Vicarage Street I'd take it out and carry it with the point of the pin just under my thumbnail. The plan was that if anybody stopped me I would jab them with it, but luckily I never met anybody!

Minnie Davies

In 1962 a chap by the name of Jones got me a job at Dales, Leominster. We were working in Craven Arms, building shutters to put concrete in. It snowed, and they put me on the dole for eleven weeks – £4 12/6 a week. Then I went back, and I was at Dales for twelve or thirteen years, putting up purlins. I wasn't very good with height, to tell the truth, so I went inside.

Arthur Edwards

Going on, I worked for the West Midland Egg Producers, at the poultry depot there. They were in Weobley, Tenbury, all over the county. They sent me to Tenbury, and when that closed down they transferred me to the poultry depot in Leominster, down Bridge Street, opposite the Garage. There were loads of chickens and turkeys coming in on a kind of belt, and I used to look away as I went through from the office; believe me, the smell was horrible. There was a lot of cruelty in those days. One driver was particularly cruel, and I had a battle royal with him on lots of occasions.

Pauline Davies

When the local abattoir was condemned and closed in 1966 or 1967 I didn't know what to do, but within a few months there came a vacancy on the local dust cart, and they offered it me. It was all dustbins then; you used to fetch the dustbins and take them back to the houses and put the lids on. I loved it because every bit of the day was outdoors. It was exceptionally hard work, but the walking suited me, and it was a carefree job – so long as you emptied your dustbins and put them back, you'd done your job. When you finished your round, you'd finished. We never stopped for rain or snow, and I never once got in the cab because it was raining.

Then I had an accident, and I found that I couldn't do the walking. It wasn't fair on the team, so I had to reluctantly go to see the boss and tell him I couldn't carry on.

Did the men of the cart belong to a union? Certainly not! There was no such thing. The bulk of Leominster Council's gang were ex-farm labourers. I can remember one morning they asked the dustmen to meet in the yard about joining a union. So we turned out, grudgingly, because we liked to get on with our round. When it was put to the vote, these old boys in the gang, the farm workers, wouldn't dare join the union. If the boss found out they were in a union they were down the bloody road! There was always plenty of people to take their place.

Malcolm Newman

There was a six weeks' postal strike in January 1971. There had been a one day strike of postmen soon after I joined, and I refused to recognise it, which made for further unpopularity with the Union of Post Office Workers. I didn't hear until years later that it was thanks to the Union Secretary at the time, Mr Ken Scandrett, that I was not thrown out of the Union. That six weeks' strike was hard to bear, as it was contrary to my nature and beliefs. After twenty-four years in the RAF saying 'Yes sir, no sir', I wasn't very

Union minded. I lost weight on that strike, with the worry and everything.

Herbert Millichamp

I came to work in Forbury House in 1982. In those days the house was all bed-sits. There was one room for the owners to live in and there was one room for residents; it was a very large room, two beds on one side of the room and two beds on the other. Burghill was the mental hospital in those days, and it was closing, so they had to get rid of all these patients. This is why homes like this opened up. We had four straight away and then we had more as the home got bigger, which happened as the bed-sits were vacated, until we had room for twenty-eight. So I've seen a lot of changes, and the house has undergone major surgery. It's an old building, three hundred years old. It's a lovely place, and it's friendly. I know where every nook and cranny is. It's a beautiful house, and I love it.

Meryl Boff

I used to go to Richards Furnishing after school to help out, you know, and then I went to work there, just helping with upholstery and things like that, helping deliver the stuff.

There were about four people working there, and Richards himself. We used to make coffins up in those days. It took about a day to make each one. We used to keep all the boards in the cellar, in the cool. The boards would come in ready cut to about the size you needed. You would trim them and put saw cuts every half an inch, then pour boiling water on to get them to bend, if you were lucky. If you were unlucky they'd break, which is an expensive game.

The shop started as Lewis's Furnishers in Broad Street. There were two brothers, and they fell out. Thomas Lewis stayed in Broad Street and Andrew Lewis started another firm up in Corn Street, and that's how it came to be split up. It was Andrew Lewis for a good many years, and then Jack Richards took it on, and changed the name to Richards. Then he retired and we took it on, and just kept the name.

When we first started we used to do upholstery and antique repairs. Old chairs and things like that. We were in one shop, and then we bought the shop next door to it and knocked it through. We could keep a lot more furniture in those days, but we got busier and busier with flooring, so eventually we gave up the woodwork and the upholstery and just concentrated on flooring and curtains, blinds, that sort of thing. Our shop is probably the longest running in the town, over a hundred years. I worked there all my working life.

Ray Watkins

Post-war developments

There were poor families, even after the war. The 'nit nurse' was always in school and they used to sit the people together who had nits on a regular basis and they put all this yellow stuff in their hair, thick yellow. It was awful, it wouldn't be allowed today.

Although you didn't have any money, you had to be respectable. You always had to look well kept. My mother always darned my jumpers, but there were people sitting in class with holes in the sleeves of their cardigans and jumpers, and some children went to school with holes in their shoes. We had the same pair of socks on until they wore out, but you washed them every night. We'd hang them in a row on the mantelpiece at night and bank the fire up so they'd dry. We always had clean socks and hankies, even my brother! We always had to be respectable.

I must have been about four or five when we moved from Etnam Street to Caswell Crescent, Caswell Road actually. It was quite a posh house then. We had our own bathroom, our own kitchen, it was lovely.

We used to swap clothes. We'd give clothes my brother grew out of to somebody else, and they'd give us clothes for my brother as he was growing. We lived next door to a very large family, and we would swap meat for something that they'd got, and that's how you got by.

It was a poor time; you had a job to survive, really. Michael Clayton came round for the rent on a Friday, and people who couldn't afford it would hide and pretend they were out. We all had gas meters, we didn't have electric. Was it one shilling or two for the meter? There was four of us, there was us, the Morrisons, there was Bargy Hughes across the road, and the Nicholas family. We used to go between each other's houses; if they hadn't got enough money for their gas meter they'd come to us, and we'd go round in a square.

The only reason we got the television was because Mum and Dad had a life insurance which matured. The Refuge man used to come round every Monday to pick up the two bob. They used to go round the houses to collect every week and they'd write it down in a little buff book. It was only pennies, but it was for your funeral. Paying for your funeral! When Mum and Dad died the policy was still there, but it wasn't even enough to buy a good wreath, yet Mum and Dad thought it was going to bury them.

Meryl Boff

People didn't want their old houses any more; they wanted new Council houses with bathrooms, which was only right. But looking back on it now, it's so sad that all those lovely little black and white cottages down the bottom end of Bridge Street went. They could have been added to – extensions and what have you – but no, they all vanished. Very sad.

Pauline Davies

When I first came to Leominster, the Birmingham Overspill Plan was about to be brought into force. All the lands from where the sewage works is now right round Cockroft and right round to New Hall Lane – that was all zoned for overspill. I remember a big public meeting in the old Town Hall to sell it to the locals. But then the government funding was moved from Leominster to Redditch and Telford, and the whole project was abandoned. Along came the developers, and they almost automatically got permission to build around the whole of that hill frontage. The Council couldn't argue that it was unsuitable for development.

Denis Turton

Behind 'Delfame' was the Pump Piece, which had an old standpipe pump in the corner, the up and down variety, with a handle. Then there was another field with a footpath running across it which we used to cross to go to school in the Bargates. The area called the Sandpit was literally sandpits at that time. We used to have great fun as children, running up and down, or sliding down them on tin trays. There was quite a lot of land around there.

The Council houses were built shortly after the war. My grandfather had promised me that I could have a pony, but before the pony materialised, he had a letter from the Council taking his land over on a compulsory purchase order. So I didn't get my pony. The whole of the Sandpit was covered by Council houses. The development gradually went on after that – first Stockenhill Road, then Newlands Drive, then the road parallel with Stockenhill.

Maureen Crumpler

Caswell Crescent

Houses in Westfield Walk under construction

We got a room or two in Burgess Street with a local chap and his wife: 'Blower' Bowen and Rose Bowen. I was earning £6 a week then, and the rent was 30 shillings, so you can tell we had hard times when we first married.

There was a little old derelict cottage going in Ryelands, where the shop used to be – Parker's. There was only one bedroom of any use, the others had all caved in. We went into this little cottage in 1952 or 1953 – we had a little girl by then. Luckily for me, three of my brothers were builders and they came and made it liveable. Within twelve to eighteen months these houses were being built, and we were allocated a house up here – this house. And lived happily ever after!

Malcolm Newman

At the time Stockenhill Road only had semi-detached houses on the left, for about probably three or four hundred yards, and then it stopped and became a dirt track lane. On the other side was The Shieling, which had a Swiss Chalet in the huge garden which had been brought from Switzerland apparently and rebuilt. I think it was possibly a Polish family who were evacuees living there, and we used to play with one of the children of the family at one time. That was a fascinating place.

Maureen Crumpler

The town was very congested. Buses used to come straight up Broad Street and through the High Street; they occasionally met in the middle. A couple of lorries meeting in the middle of the High Street caused chaos. So there was a planning enquiry about the new road, the present ring road. After it was planned

I represented quite a few objectors and people who wanted to be heard. I made the longest speech of my life – a day and a bit! I had to deal with the whole of the route, dealing with each objection all the way round. There was no objection to the road, we really wanted a road, but there were minor matters. Of course we're glad we've got it now.

Denis Turton

The Inner Relief Road was a blessing. That took a tremendous amount of traffic out of the centre. And when the A49 was cut through, that was a marvellous success.

Alec Haines

The Swiss Chalet at The Shieling

There was a lot of children after the war, so I'm part of the baby boom. There was three classes in each age group in the Secondary School. 1a1, 1a2, 1a3 and 1ba1, 1ba2, 1ba3, where normally there was only 1a or 1b. The children were all separated by age. If your birthday came between December and April you went into one class and that how it was divided. Nothing to do with your skills or anything like that. We just touched on everything: cooking, needlework, half an hour sewing and that kind of thing. PE was one hour per week. It was homework all the time in those days. You had to wear a uniform and if I can remember, it was very expensive. You just had one shirt, one jumper, one tie, you had one of everything and you had to look after it. I got on really well there, I took to needlework and I made a dress with box pleats; it was very complicated, and I had to model it in front of the school.

Meryl Boff

We were amongst the first to go to the Secondary School at Church Street, and they extended it in Green Lane where we had the ex-army huts. We had these huts that the soldiers had had during the war. The stoves were the same – the coke fire in the middle of the classroom – unless you were huddled all over them, you got no heat. It was hard going; it really was, because it was so cold, it was horrible. But there were more things going on than at Miss Thomas's.

I had my very first trip abroad in 1950 to Switzerland, Lugarno. We went there with the school for two weeks. Stayed in Dover the night, and then by train into Switzerland. We stayed at like a Youth Hostel. It was beautiful, it really was. And there was Gandria, a little island. Of course we'd never had an experience anything like that. The soldiers were the only ones that ever went abroad. It was great. And we went to the Festival of Britain in 1951, that was a wonderful experience. The Skylon was made at Painters in Hereford, and Jimmy Williams, my aunty's husband, brought it from Hereford to the Festival.

Pauline Davies

Maypole to Rock and Roll

For the Coronation in 1953 they had a maypole in the Crescent. All the children had a piece of ribbon and as we ran around we made a plait round the maypole.

Meryl Boff

One of our favourite games in the summer holidays was a game called garden sneaking. We'd usually play from about six o'clock till about eight. There'd be about thirty of us, half of us going to hide, and then the other half going looking. It was called garden sneaking because we used to sneak in everybody's back garden! You usually picked the ones with fruit trees in, pears and apples and all that. I loved it. Mind, we used to get told off. We didn't do malicious damage but you'd tuck up in a garden, dive over somebody's fence, and knock over somebody's fruit. But it was the thing, that's what we used to do.

Tony Rock

I wasn't very old, couldn't have been five, and we used to go blackberry picking, and pick as many blackberries as we could. Neesham's Garage at the bottom of Etnam Street, he used to buy them off us for next to nothing, just pennies really.

Meryl Boff

We used to go all over the place to catch fish, especially up the back of The Sands, and going up for about three or four miles up to Kingsland on the Lugg. At that time it used to meander beautifully, and then over the years the alleviation scheme for the floods straightened it out. At that time a lot of the stretch of the river belonged to the Bright family. They had the butcher's shop up in the High Street and they used to let us fish there. We spent many happy hours up there and caught loads of fish. What we didn't eat, we used to take to John Wright, who had a greengrocer's and grocer's in Corn Street. There was no fishmongers as such, but John was always willing to buy the fish off the lads.

In the summer we spent hours on the Worcester Road bridge, because it's got those little indents for pedestrians. We used to fish off there, probably every night, of the summer holidays. Maggots cost a lot of money, so we used wasp grubs. We used to get stung to death to get them, but they were great fishing bait.

Tony Rock

We moved into Leominster and stayed with friends who had The Bell in Etnam Street. I used to collect all these bottle tops, and I used to take bottles back and get money back on them, things like that. Anyway, while we lived in the pub my brother and I had to share a room. We were supposed to be in bed asleep, my mum didn't know what we were doing. We used to listen to them coming out after they'd been drinking and we'd get these coins and let them down on a piece of string, and rattle them. You couldn't afford to lose money then, and they'd be out on the pavement striking their matches to try and find the coin. They never found out what we were doing, but we had to be careful not do it all the time.

Lee McColgan

I always thought the town was divided, to be honest with you. We called the area from the hospital in South Street up towards Churchill Avenue, Shanghai. We weren't allowed to talk to people who lived up Shanghai; don't ask me why, I could never understand it. We weren't really allowed to mix, but what we did as kids was to meet in the Grange and play fox and hounds. Not just one or two, I'm talking about thirty or forty children. We'd pinch Mum's chalk ornaments from the bedroom, because we needed chalk for the game. We divided up into two teams. Up Shanghai they were always older children, and the children from the Crescent and Etnam Street were always younger. We would have chalk arrows round the Grange and the Sydonia; we thought nobody knew about it. Everybody had a whale of a time, and it used to go on for hours, this game. Just with a piece of chalk. Of course they knew where we were, because they used to follow the arrows! Nobody had enough sense to wipe them off. Every time we played this game we always used up a complete ornament.

Meryl Boff

The Reverend Evans ran the Youth Club down Etnam Street. He used to take us to places like Bosbury, Worcester, all over, to this square dancing. That was about the limit of it for our age group! The Youth Club was very well attended. All we had was a wind up gramophone, table tennis, darts, and that was about it. We made our entertainment, we loved it, it was wonderful. That and the cinema that was in Leominster, there was nothing else. We weren't allowed to go into pubs or anything like that, even in my 20s. You just were not allowed to go.

Pauline Davies

The Youth Club used to be in Etnam Street, in the Orphans Home, it was very popular. Then the Hereford and Worcester Council built us a new Youth Club down just below where the latest swimming pool is. Well, you'd probably get a hundred or more kids every night, with Mr Burke, Dicky Burke, one of the former Mayors and Councillors. But sadly that's all gone, that used to be a great place. They catered for everything, and it was very well run. The original Youth Club was more like a National Association of Boys Club; you had a lot of the police officers there, coaching table tennis, boxing and stuff like that, and you had all the playing fields there, hockey and football.

Tony Rock

They also had the Institute and Circle Club, at the 'Stute'. A chap there called Peter Budd did most of the running of it, and he taught us to dance. It was only boys there, and he used to put these records on, and we used to hold a chair! The Institute and Circle had a proper dance floor, and they had the Circle Six Band

160

on a Saturday night. A lot of local people used to be in the band, looking ever so smart, and they'd play quicksteps, waltzes, and foxtrots, and jive as well, and it was very popular. They used to get a lot from the RAF camp at Credenhill on a Saturday night. That was practically it as far as Saturday night entertainment went.

They had dances at Orleton, and Kingsland when they built the Coronation Hall. They ran a bus there and a bus back. If you didn't catch the bus, you had to walk. That was it; there was no second bus. It wasn't so far to walk from Kingsland, it's only three miles.

Ray Fisher

I loved the dances. We used to go to Kingsland and Orleton. Kingsland was more dressed-up dancing, whereas Orleton was rock and roll. You wore your jeans, it was real rock and roll, the 50s. There'd be two buses. At Kingsland we had the No Name Trio. There was George Colley and Terry Postings, who played the accordion, they made some good music. In the interval at Kingsland we'd have half an hour of rock and roll; other than that it was all ballroom dancing. The village hall at Orleton was an old tin shack! Mr Lee we used to call him, and he had this old record player thing, but did we have some fun there! You knew it was rock and roll all night!

The Church Institute (The Stute) in South Street. It was demolished in the late 1960s to make way for the British Legion

It depended on what sort of mood you were in or who was going. Is somebody special going there? Are we going to meet some nice boys? Where are the best boys going to be tonight, should we go this way or that way? Sometimes, if you were dressed to go to one place, it was difficult to decide to go to the other one; you sort of had to stick with it. That was our Saturday night thing.

Lee McColgan

Even the Beatles played at Tenbury Wells, when they were called the Silver Beetles. There's a lot of Leominster people who actually went to the Bridge that night. I was stood outside, thinking who are they? They didn't sound very good, they had a couple of little amplifiers between them. I remember looking through the window and seeing John Lennon, Paul McCartney, George Harrison and Stuart Sutcliffe.

Leominster was blessed with a lot of good musicians in the late 50s and 60s. Bands like The Buddies, Barry Tyrol, Terry Tyrol, and Reggie Sage played at dances. You had Phil and the Vampires, or was it Phil and the Phantoms? There was a band at the Grammar school called JJ Rip, from their initials, John, Jim, Russell, Ian, and Peter. I thought to myself, I can do that, so at the end of term do, we gave it a go. All we had was one Spanish guitar between us, and we did the Troggs song 'Love is all around'. Before I knew it I'd got roped into singing in this band, I was only thirteen. We used to pay half a crown to practise in Monkland Village Hall on a Thursday night. We started from there and we were quite good actually.

George Colley took over from Mr Miles as the manager of the old Clifton cinema, and he allowed us to practise on a Sunday morning. In return for having free use, we'd have to put all the stuff up for the cinema, or later the bingo. They also let us play at some Friday night venues. Rock and roll between the pictures, it was brilliant.

The old Clifton cinema was a good venue for wrestling. A lot of them were recorded, but they weren't shown on telly, when you had the wrestling on ITV television, with Kent Walton and all those. You had the famous Jackie Palo, Mick McManus and all of them.

We had a contract with the Flamingo in Hereford, long closed now. We played every other Friday, and we supported the acts. I met a lot of interesting people – the Beach Boys from America, Reg Pressley, Dave Dee, the Troggs, the Marmalade lads, Dean Ford, when they first had their big hits. It was the birthplace of a lot of bands, like Slade, when they were just starting. I could have ended up making a living at it, but I didn't. A lot of the time the money was terrible. We used to go Rednal Social Club in Birmingham, a top venue, for £15 a night between five of us!

Tony Rock

They used to have these big stars in the cinema in Leominster. Dennis Lotus, Lita Rosa, George Hamilton IV, and Eddie Calvert – oh goodness me! I found out they were coming from somewhere, got in the middle of the road and stopped the car they were in. I was supposed to be at work in the office, but I was there out on the road to meet them.

Lee McColgan

Just after the Second world War, and well into the sixties until they finished the cricket there was a little shop in the corner of the Grange run by Clive Morris and his partner, who had the chip shop in Etnam Street, selling drinks and what have you.

For the Leominster Evening News Cup, they used to have teams from Worcester, Ludlow, and Kington. It was a brilliant venue. Some very famous cricketers played on that pitch. The Richardson brothers who played cricket for England used to play for Kington. Robbie Richardson was that quick you couldn't see the ball – and that was in really good daylight in the summer. There used to be metal bars which protected the corner near Grange House. Bargy Hughes told us that all the lads who used to watch the cricket in the area would swing on the bars, and all the money would fall out of their pockets. He knew it'd be down in the grass. We used to find threepenny bits, tanners, even half crowns. That was my spending money for the week.

Tony Rock

Oh yes, the Grange made Leominster an attraction. But someone struck a ball and it hit a car in the car park and broke a window, and then the insurance company would not insure. An alternative ground was found near where the Leisure Centre is, by the Minster College, but nobody went there to watch cricket, and it went to the Leisure Centre at Bridge Street. Nobody goes down there. It was so convenient on the Grange. You could buy a bag of chips on Corn Square and enjoy them while watching the game. Or after the game you could buy your chips, then go somewhere and have a drink. It was so close to the centre of town. You could come to do some shopping and watch for half an hour before the bus went, just right. It should never have been abandoned, and is sorely missed.

Mervyn Bufton

Children playing cricket on the Grange

Children returning from the Grange to the junior school

We used to have the Life Boys and the Boys Brigade meetings, Tuesday and Fridays at the Moravian Church. George Warburton was the Captain; he lived just across the road. We were the First Battalion, and a few years later the Reverend at the Methodist Church in Green Lane opened up the Second Battalion. I didn't know much about that, but at one time the First Battalion was the biggest in Herefordshire.

I joined Life Boys, which is the Junior organisation. I remember that one of the very first times I went to the senior Boys' Brigade was the night of the Aberfan disaster in Wales. The Reverend Cooper was the vicar then at the Moravian, and he sat us down and told us what had happened. We just said prayers, and then we went upstairs and did our stuff. It was a lot more military than the Scouts. You did a lot of religion – Bible class – and community stuff as well. It was the first time I ever learned to fold a shirt tidy! We had summer camps in Leintwardine, and a band, which played at a lot of the Remembrance Parades. It was great, I loved it. I wish the Boys Brigade was still going now, because I think it would be a great thing for the kids.

Tony Rock

I used to go to the Brownies. They had a little hut behind the Greens, and I had to remember a pencil, a bit of string, and a notepad. The Brownies used to put a float into the Carnival and one year I was an owl, and I was also a pixie to Father Christmas!

Lindsey Murray

There were two Cub packs in the town in the 1970s. They met on two separate nights down at the Scout Hall, which is down the dead end part of Pinsley Road. I think there were probably about 25 cubs in each pack, which for a town this size was quite a lot. They were both very good Cub packs and they both thrived.

My first real involvement was when they proposed that there should be a Gang Show. Every single Scout and Cub was told they were in it – they had no choice! Every Sunday afternoon, we were all down the Scout Hall for it must have been about three months, rehearsing. All the Cubs from both packs, one Scout troop and all the Scouters, and various mums and dads helping. The dads made the scenery, and the mums made the costumes. It was a really social gathering – it was a tie, as it was every Sunday, but it was quite good fun really.

For the shows we used the main hall at the Minster School on Thursday, Friday, Saturday, and it was done during the Easter holidays. It took all day, from about ten in the morning, and it was chaos, absolute chaos. When I think back, it's amazing that the show ever got off the ground, really, but it was good.

The Scouts used to do the Leominster Post at Christmas. They copied that off the Hereford Scouts. Various shops in town and the supermarkets would have special post boxes. You popped your local cards and your money in the box and then on the Sunday before Christmas they would collect them all up, take them to the Scout Hall and sort them, and then the Scouts would deliver them round the town. So all that money was profit. They still do that; it must have been going for thirty years.

Gwenda Causer

Personalities of Leominster

In Etnam Street, when I was a young fellow, was the Waverley Hotel (opposite to where the Waverley is now). I can picture it now – the steps and the green doors. One of the residents was a man named Stosher Wood – 'Stosher' was a nickname, I should think. I don't think he had any family and he lived at the Waverley. He was upwards of six feet tall, ex-Army I should think, a smart chap, with a moustache. He was getting on then, and he'd ridden in the Grand National once as an amateur. When it was bitter cold, icy, he'd go down over the bridge and swim in the river, in the early morning.

Malcolm Newman

I do remember the gentleman who gave us the playing field [Stanley Holland], I remember his funeral. The schoolchildren had to wear black and white dresses, and we made a guard of honour down either side, and he was taken and buried behind a shelter in the old playing field. (The shelter's gone now.) I believe I've got a mug here; we were all given mugs to commemorate it.

Minnie Davies

Charlie Acton was a Friday character. He always emerged on market day and he used to wear bizarre clothes and a top hat, and direct the traffic. I don't think they'd put up with that today. Everybody knew Charlie Acton, he was harmless. I suppose you'd call him a character.

Ray Fisher

I remember Charlie Acton – the little man who'd stand in the road directing the traffic. There were two or three places where you were likely to see him. He used to wear a top hat, but he also had a white pith helmet which he wore on occasions. The one thing you had to be careful not to do was follow his directions on the traffic. You had to make your own observations. He wasn't always wrong, but if you relied on him you were asking for trouble.

Denis Turton

There were so many characters around the town. There was Billy Blunt – he didn't work, but when there was a sale he used to drive the cattle down to the station, odd jobs like that. When I was a kid he was well known in the town as a character. So was Mr Thomas, who kept the Talbot at one time. He was a bit of a wild one. He used to have a chap working for him, and I saw him and this chap going like billy-oh. He used to get after him.

They used to have trucks with loads of coal coming in to the sidings here, and the coalman used to go and collect it and deliver it on drays, you know, horse-drawn drays. There was one coalman – we called him 'Nubbly Ones', because he had little nubbly coal. Mr Bott was another one. He didn't go round; he had an office in the station yard. My grandfather worked for 'The Old Radnor Trading Company', which was taken over later on by a firm called Blake's. They had a chap in the office taking orders and doing the books, and my grandfather used to unload these railway trucks onto the vehicles that had come to collect the coal. That was hard work.

Fred Parsons

In his youth Stanley Holland worked for Leominster Corporation, but he was caught stealing and had to leave the town. He emigrated to America, where he made his fortune. He never forgot his home town, and made large donations to its charities. He became the first freeman of Leominster, and his funeral at the Priory Church was conducted by the Bishop of Hereford

I don't know if you've heard of Tom the milkman? In the war, I used to have a drop of milk off him, we all did. He'd wheel this iron truck; you could hear him a mile off! I would leave my money in the milk jug. He would leave his cans up the street – one can full of milk in one street, and another in another street. If it was raining the boys used to open them. They used to play some pranks, mind!

Margery Hunt

Tom the milkman always had a can with his milk in, and the boys used to take the lid off and put stuff in, and then put the lid back on. I said to Mum not ever to buy any of that milk! When Tom's horse died he had a little cart, it was like thrown together, all odd bits of wood, to carry his urns around.

Eileen Bacon

Tom used to walk round the town with a little pushcart to carry his milk. The number of his customers went down and down, but he still had a few customers left when he gave it up. Then I discovered that a number of people in the town who were his past customers had continued taking milk from him, one or two pints a week, which they poured down the drain. You couldn't drink any milk that he delivered, but they kept it up for old time's sake. We didn't know of any relatives, so when the old man died I was one of his executors, perhaps the only one. When we went to his house to clear it up it was chock full of books and newspapers. For years he'd gone to the Russell, Baldwin and Brights book sales, and if there was one book he liked, he'd buy the bundle. He'd take out the book he wanted, and the rest of the books in the bundle

Tom Williams, the Midnight Milkman, by Marjorie Cook

just stayed piled up in his house. Quite literally everywhere was full of books and newspapers of all sorts. They were even piled on the stairs, leaving just enough room to go by one step at a time. In his bedroom, one side of the bed was piled up with books.

Denis Turton

My uncle was Bill Ladd, they all knew him. He worked at the gas works, he was a stoker in the furnaces, and he was a bit of a case. He did shift work in the Torches and I used to take his tea, all the fires going.

His mother and father died, and he made his home with my dad. He used to sleep in a little covered room outside the kitchen in the summer. It was like a little house! All on its own. Mum didn't like him smoking his pipe in the house, but he could out there.

He used to tell me some tales. One day I asked him, 'Uncle Bill, have you ever been to the seaside?' 'Yes, I have,' he said, 'and I missed the train. Anyhow, this whale come up and he said "Are you Bill Ladd from Leominster?" And he opened his mouth and said, "Jump in then and I'll take you home!"' We used to sit open-mouthed. He gave us a penny every Friday when he had his money. If it was nearing Christmas, we'd put a ha'penny up and spend a ha'penny.

He always drank at the Red Lion, in Bridge Street. Nobody was allowed to sit on his chair. 'Don't sit there, that's Bill Ladd's chair!'

Margery Hunt

Buff Ainsley was the window cleaner in Leominster for years and years. He had a little pencil-thin moustache, and he was always very smart. He had tatty trousers, but a really posh jacket and a trilby. He always tipped his hat to all the ladies – he thought he was a ladies' man. People used to say he couldn't possibly clean the windows properly, being so smartly dressed. But he was a nice old boy. He could play the guitar beautifully; I think he taught himself. To earn extra money he used to teach guitar playing in the evenings. He taught quite a few people in Leominster.

He used to live down past the Priory Church, those little cottages down on the left, and whenever he saw me he gave me a penny. He was always up ladders but tipping his hat to any lady that went past. How he cleaned the windows I'll never know. But he was well known in the town, a smart upright gentleman, ladders under one arm.

Meryl Boff

This old lady, Kitty her name was, she lived down the bottom of Bridge Street. She wasn't married; she and her brother lived together. You'd see her going off with her little basket, to get some nettles, to boil them and drink the water. She used to go and collect things out of the hedge and things out of the river, to boil and eat them. Chaps used to pull her brother's leg: 'What d'you have for tea last night, George? Boiled nettles, was it?' But they both lived to a good old age anyhow.

Margery Hunt

My father, Jack Stewart, had three garages, in Dilwyn, Docklow and Leominster, where he also had a blacksmith's shop with the garage. Then we moved to Eaton Hill, He had everything going on there, that's where everything was centred. He had Mr Chiswick the mechanic, who was brilliant. He had welders, blacksmiths and mechanics – lots of them were Polish, and they were very clever. In the 50s there were two Nissen huts in the grounds and a whole crew of Irish men came to live in them.

We had a lane at Eaton Hill, where he kept chickens and turkeys. It was coming near Christmas and they were getting stolen. He used to sit up in the bedroom in the dark with his 12 bore, and he said 'If I see anyone with a torch up that lane, they're dead!' I did worry about that. I knew when he was coming home at night from Leominster. He always had noisy powerful

Right: Jack Stewart, with his boar's head mascot. He was called Bill Bendix because he looked like the American actor.
Above: The house at Eaton Hill, complete with stock cars and chickens

cars, there were no silencers then, and you could hear the revving up, and the rrrrrrooooaaaarrrrr as he came up the drive; all the chippings would be flying.

He used to go to the auction rooms and come back with a lorryload of stuff. Beautiful, some of it. Swords and shields, carved massive mirrors, we even had tiger skins, a couple with heads on.

He didn't care what people thought of him. He could speak very nicely, but if he was in a bad mood, his language was disgusting. They went to a fancy dress ball at Kingsland and he just went in his ordinary clothes because he couldn't be bothered to dress up. He used to wear a tie to keep his trousers up, he was so scruffy. He won first prize as a tramp – they thought he was in fancy dress!

He kept pigs, and he'd spend a lot of time down there scratching their backs and making sure they didn't get burnt when it was hot. He went bankrupt when I was away, and the pigs had swine fever, and he lost them all. That really broke his heart.

When Bill Bendix retired the sport was never quite the same again. For his going signified the end of an era. Let us be frank, there were many who cheered when Bill decided to call it a day. If you remember Bill Bendix you will cheer when you see him, although you might have booed him once upon a time. It was men like these, tough men, hard living, hard driving men who settled their grievances on the track and raced for the hell of it who built up the sport.

Programme for Bradfield Stadium Stock Car Meeting,
May 1965

Stock car racing was his other love. It was a big thing then, they were drawing big crowds. He used to get paid an extra £10 for every car he turned over! He didn't care about the money, he just enjoyed turning them over. If he destroyed a car he'd give them the money to get another one. He was a good sport, but some of them didn't treat it like a sport. Once they set one of his cars on fire in the pits, and he had to have police protection.

In 1954 he won the Herefordshire Sportsman of the Year. The salver is inscribed 'Jack Stewart – "William Bendix" 1954'.

He loved being a publican. He had the Brickmakers on Barons Cross Road. Well, it wasn't his; it was his wife's (she was my step-mum) – it had been in her family for years. Coachloads would follow him to the meeting tracks, and coaches would often come to the Brickmakers to see the well known character. When he was at the pub with my step-mum they used to do breakfasts for people passing by. Ham and eggs, he'd say – not bacon and eggs, always ham and eggs.

The day of his funeral, I've never seen anything like it in Leominster. The whole town came to a standstill. In those days men took off their caps, you know and bowed their heads as the hearse went by, it was amazing. And the cemetery – well, I've never seen so many wreaths in my life. It was absolutely covered. It was very moving.

Lee McColgan

Jack Peatt was quite a character. Apparently at one time he was the Governor General of one of the islands – the Philippines or somewhere out that way. Then they came back and he was a practising vet. He had racehorses, and he won the Lincoln in 1969 with a horse called Ben Nevis, ridden by a jockey from Ludlow. All the local lads had money on it, and he won. Everybody went down there for the next few nights, and they were singing 'Well done' outside in the street. Mrs Peatt was a JP, and sponsored a lot of things in the town. She supported the almshouses in Bargates, and a lot of charities.

Mr Peatt eventually went blind. He was once in Hereford Hospital, and the story went that the nurses had smuggled in a copy of the *Sporting Life* for him, and he found out that his horse was running at Yarmouth that day. Hereford to Yarmouth is a long way! But he got there, apparently, and Lester Piggott was riding the horse. They were really good characters for Leominster. A lot of Leominster people loved them to bits, and still talk about them.

Tony Rock

My dad, John Pugh, was born in Etnam Street, when they had the shoe shop there. He took it over when his dad died, and the shop was his life; he just lived and breathed shoes. He would walk down the street looking at people's feet and their shoes, and he knew everybody's shoe size that came into the shop. We didn't have many holidays, and if we did go, we had to go on a Sunday and come back on a Thursday because of the weekend. He even married Mum on a Thursday afternoon because it was half-day closing and he didn't have to shut the shop to marry her!

He always let people take shoes out – never took a deposit for them, just signed them off in the book. They took them home at the weekend, tried them and brought them back the next week. Some farmers would only pay once a year. They'd come in and put their shoes, their kids' shoes, their boots and Wellingtons, in the

John Pugh

book. The first week in January we'd send them a bill, they'd come in and pay it, and that was it.

Slippers were the main thing at Christmas, weren't they? A lady used to ring up and ask for twenty-odd pairs of slippers. She'd give Dad the list and he'd sort them out, pack them up and in the corner of each parcel he'd put the name and size. She'd pick them up and then pay for them after Christmas. That was how she did her Christmas shopping for years.

There's a chap in Leominster who would buy Dad a whisky every time he saw him. He said, 'If it hadn't been for you helping my mum out, we'd have had no shoes.' Dad just let people have shoes and pay for them when they could afford it, and then he'd knock a bit off. He always got the money in the end. A lot of people have said since he died that if it wasn't for him they wouldn't have had shoes when they were children. Quite nice really, isn't it?

When Dad was ill, so many people used to come in and ask how he was that in the end I wrote a bulletin on the chalk board outside the shop, where I used to put the prices. But it still didn't stop people from coming in to ask about him.

Dad loved his sport – rugby, cricket and football – but he had polio, so he could only play skittles. He played at the Rankin Club for The Cobblers for fifty years. They arranged a presentation at the Club for him, a silver tray with his name on, but he passed away on the Sunday. We all agreed as a family to go and pick it up for him.

With Charles Winston, the club steward, he arranged for a Welsh Male Voice Choir to sing at the Rankin Club every year. Their twenty-fourth year was the year that Dad died, and they sang at his funeral. That year they also sang at a concert I organised at the Priory Church for the Charles Renton Unit Appeal, and they're going to come back every year to do concerts in the Priory. It'll be twenty-seven years this year, and it all started with Dad.

Denise Pugh

Edie Newman

Edie Newman was something of a pioneer. She had a son, Geoffrey, who had learning disabilities, and when he came of school age she was incensed by the lack of facilities for him in the area. In November 1964, she attended the inaugural meeting of the North Herefordshire Society for Learning Difficulties and was made Honorary Secretary. So began the long fight for equality for people with learning difficulties.

It was not long before a house in Pump Piece became what would be described in today's parlance as a Care Home. In 1977, another house was rented from the Council and became home to several residents. This spread to another house, much of the early expense being met by Edie.

At the top of her garden she had a workshop, where the residents could carry out craft activities and games in the daytime. Through her foresight, and the bravery of Herefordshire County Council, care in the community was thus established, long before any Government hijacked the idea.

She received an MBE for her work. Since her untimely death in 1999 her family have continued with her request that the Care Homes continue to provide a home for life for the existing residents.

Les Newman and the residents of Pump Piece

I became the Superintendent Registrar, and all the old registers in the safe had to be moved up to 38 South Street. We tried to get one of the professional safe-moving firms, but the then County Council would not pay their fee. So with John Croft's help we got together a gang. Alexander and Duncan provided a low loader, and we went down to the back entrance to the bank in Burgess Street to get the safe out. As we were bringing one safe out from the back door to the lorry on rollers, I was putting one of the rollers under the trolley for the next two or three feet of movement when one of the chaps holding the safe up on crowbars dropped his crowbar, and they dropped the safe. I lost the tip of my finger, but it wasn't very serious; the only trouble was it stopped me playing the violin.

Denis Turton

I was on the Town Council for twenty-five years, and twenty-seven on the District. As an Independent, I didn't have to look over my shoulder, and I did everything I could for Leominster, as I've done all my life. I was in two orphanages, one in Leominster, and a big one at Bristol. I've been made an honorary Alderman, whatever that means, I've been Mayor of Leominster three times, and I've had the great privilege of being invited to the garden parties at Buckingham Palace on two occasions.

Alec Haines

Arty Bishop, one of our neighbours, was on the District and Town Council, and encouraged me to stand. My husband was already on the Council and I used to be at home taking the phone calls and sorting everything out so it really wasn't new to me. I put up in 1987 and I've been on there ever since. In 1994 I was deputy mayor to Alec Haines, who deserves the title of 'Mr Leominster', and in 1994-95 I was the 445th Mayor since 1554. My Mayor-making took place at the Talbot Hotel, and I was proud of that, because my mother worked there when I was a child in Leominster.

One of the first engagements was at Brierley Court Farm, where I planted an oak tree. That was the first of 363 engagements that year, sometimes five in one day. It was a huge commitment; it was invitations all the time. The money I was given for expenses went within a matter of weeks because there was such a lot going on. Prizes were wanted everywhere – can you contribute this and that? In my year the Mayor's Fund raised £10,000. Macmillan Nurses had the majority, and the local Scouts, Guides and Brownies had the rest. The one disappointment was the closure of our last grocer's shops in the High Street during that year. That was a very sad thing.

Pauline Davies

The Historical Society was formed first. One of the first lectures was at the Oak, given by Lord Rennell of Rodd. I remember it quite distinctly. At regular intervals during the lecture he produced a large red silk handkerchief out of his breast pocket draped it over his arm, picked up a snuff box, had a sniff, blew his nose, put the handkerchief back and continued with his lecture. I got to know Lord Rennell quite well later on.

Three or four of us decided to see what we could do about perpetuating the study of Leominster history. The leading light of the group was Norman Reeves; then there was Margaret Davies, wife of Norman Davies, and Elizabeth Thomas, and a Mr Barrow. We had a meeting in my office simply because it was a convenient place. The result was that I got landed as chairman of the society, Barrow became treasurer, and Norman Davies became secretary.

We managed to buy the premises for the museum with the help of a bank loan, and subscribers who bought a brick each, and functions and lectures, all sort of money-raising ventures.

Denis Turton

John Cross and his wife, Norman Davies and his wife, and Norman Reeves, who wrote *The Town in the Marches*, were all very much involved in setting up the museum. I started later, helping the curator with various things and writing little pamphlets. Then she wanted to give up and eventually I took over. I was a bit reluctant; it wasn't my sort of thing, really. I spent most of my time worrying about the building. I can vividly remember our treasurer

LEOMINSTER MUSEUM PROJECT

A

PUBLIC MEETING

will be held at

the Royal Oak Hotel, Leominster

on

MONDAY, 20ᵗʰ JULY, 1970

at 8 p.m.

(Chairman: His Worship The Mayor, Alderman Norman Davies)

To discuss the formation of a Leominster Museum and to elect a Committee

PLEASE SUPPORT THIS PROJECT

coming in to a committee meeting and saying, 'You might not believe this, but we are actually solvent!' That was the first time the museum had paid off all its outstanding debts. Since then, touch wood, we've always been just about in the black.

Local history introduced me to lots of nice people, and it's involved me in things I never thought I'd be involved in at all. I did a recording for BBC Woman's Hour with a lady who'd been ducked on the Ducking Stool, and if somebody had told me twenty-five years ago that I'd spend the afternoon filming with Rik Mayall in Leominster Priory I'd have said they were nuts!

Eric Turton

Last words

In school you were aware that some children weren't very well provided for, and their clothes were ragged, because their parents were poor. I suppose generally speaking my family were not flush by any means, but you know, similar to other families. All the parents sought to do the very best for their children.

Doug Lewis

There didn't seem to be as much fear of things when I was a child as there is now. We had the soldiers, the camps, right by us in Etnam Street, but there was never the fear of anything nasty, never. We used to look after the soldiers' dogs, and there was never anything amiss.

I had a wonderful childhood. We had freedom in those days, we were allowed out. We'd go up on Eaton Hill; we had our dens up there. We'd take our bottle of pop and sandwiches, we'd go for the whole day, and nobody used to worry about us. No one was afraid, not our mothers, nor anyone. It was wonderful.

Pauline Davies

The family was everything. It was everything. There was Betty and Dolly the twins, Hazel, me and Evelyn. We always went out together, never went out without each other. Evelyn was the baby.

We used to grumble about having to take her with us, but we took her just the same. We were really close. And very happy, thank goodness.

Eileen Bacon

My memory of Leominster in the 1940s is of a small market town of about 5,000 inhabitants split into the 'haves' and the 'have-nots', where everyone in each level of society knew one another – or thought they did. Due to its location deep in the Marches and well away from any major town or city, it was pretty much isolated and backward in its agriculture and industry. The majority of people in the town were poor working class with large families, and they struggled to make ends meet. Life for the poor or underprivileged was hard, and it was almost impossible for them to break out of their class. There was, however, a feeling of togetherness amongst those people and this was never stronger than when they were singing on the way back from the hop fields. Overall the town was a happy place, with such things as cricket in the Grange, point to point horse races, and concerts in the hall of the old junior school.

Roy Gough

When I look back on our younger days in the 30s and 40s, and then I think what Leominster is now – a prosperous place with many, many incomers, I'm amazed. There we were back then, living on coppers. One day they'd want Father to work, then for the next fortnight they wouldn't want him, and he'd be back on the bit of dole you could get. Leominster now compared with how it was then – it's two completely different stories, the difference is absolutely uncanny. Leominster was so poor; people just don't know how poor it was. Only those of us who are still alive and went through it really know.

Malcolm Newman

People seemed to be a community and got on well together. They were all very friendly, and would talk to one another. People didn't move. The same folks were there for years and years. Yet most of the youngsters did move away. Not many friends of mine in those days stayed here. Most of them have gone all over the country.

Ray Watkins

When the cattle market moved out of Leominster, that took a lot of farmers out of town. They used to come in to market; the wives would come into town and do their shopping, then walk back up to the Black Swan. Then the market went, and trade in Leominster did go downhill.

Denise Pugh

Leominster was a sleepy little market town, really. Everybody knew everybody, and life went at a much slower pace than it does these days. I always seem to remember the nice days, rambling over Eaton Hill, one of our favourite places, if we weren't playing cricket or football at the Grange.

The town's got bigger, and people don't seem to meet in the middle like they used to. Everybody seems to be more spread out, doing their own thing.

I suppose basically Leominster was an agricultural town. Most people seemed to find work. Dales was a big employer in Leominster, as it is now. It was one of the main ones. There were the factories: Switchgear, those kind of places. I don't suppose it was the best paid work around. It was based on an agricultural society, so wages were automatically lower. If you lived in Hereford it might have been a little bit more, and if you lived in Birmingham it would probably have been a lot more. But I think people were quite happy with their lot round here. There's a lot to be said for living in Leominster.

Ray Fisher

Index

bb 07